T0078071

An inspiring and informative must-read book diarizing Peter Nieman's performance mindset and physical journey over 100 marathons.

-John Stanton C.M. LLD(Hon) CEO & Founder Running Room Inc. Coin des Coureurs Inc.

Each of us is running a life race, one that resembles a marathon in so many ways. With captivating stories, and profound life insights at the end of each chapter, Dr. Peter Nieman transports you into an enriched interpretation of your own race, and how to finish as a transformed, overcoming champion. The unforgettable wisdom in 101 Finish Lines, encapsulated through a commensurate number of mini chapters representing unique life experiences, is an inspirational resource guide you will return to over and over again. This cherished book will provide you with invaluable counsel and encouragement as you continue to run your personal marathon with the finish line ahead of you!

-Dr. Len Zoeteman PhD., founder Loveway.ca

101 Finish Lines tells stories of resilience, rituals, and Dr. Nieman's quest to conquer over 100 marathons. It will inspire the reader to love their life in ways that will pivot them toward their own finish lines in this journey called life.

-Adam Markel, TEDx Speaker, author of *Pivot, The I Love My Life Challenge* and host of The Conscious Pivot Podcast

This book holds the stories of every marathon Peter and I have ever completed. Ok, I only did one, but it's in the book. So are Dr. Nieman's stories of the marathon of life - with all the pain, wisdom, and humour that comes with it. A great companion to life.

-Dave Kelly, former host of Breakfast TV and co-founder of Kelly Brothers Productions

Almost There was the title Dr. Peter Nieman was considering for his book, *101 Finish Lines*. As he would finish a marathon, he would hear the chants of *Almost There*. He realized people would cheer for us—we are not alone, and that our attitude—right thinking—would get us to the finish line.

As he did with his first book, *Moving Forward,* Dr. Nieman collected wisdom spanning time and the globe. From Buddha to Dr. Gerald Jampolsky to strangers. From South Africa, Canada, America, and Europe, *101 Finish Lines* is relevant. It is not a novel or book to read to pass the time, but an inspiration to be digested daily. A lesson a day. A book for your nightstand.

-Sharon L. Hicks, author of *How Do You Grab a Naked Lady?*

If you are seeking inspiration, motivation, vision, and endurance, you will find it all here. Dr. Peter Nieman's vast experience running many marathons has yielded him the most profound insights in how to master the run of life, and he generously shares them all here. I was touched and uplifted by these shining gems of wisdom, which you can easily apply to any goal important to you. Thank you, Dr. Nieman, for your dedication to make life better, stronger, and more rewarding for all of your readers! Your life is your gift to the world.

-Alan Cohen, bestselling author of *A Deep Breath of Life*

Dr. Peter Nieman's book, *101 Finish Lines*, shows his creativity and passion for health and wellness hundreds of times. Dr. Nieman is my friend and I have had the great fortune of jogging with him several times over the years, even though we live thousands of miles apart. Every jog showed me what passion for life really means and how jogging can contribute to that. This book shows his creativity and incredible vision: he sees things that most of us cannot see and fortunately enjoys sharing those remarkable images of life and love. In this book, he does note some of the keys to success in all athletic endeavors like "never quit," "customize rituals," and "press forward." Dr. Nieman shows in this wonderful book that research on expert performance (sports, chess, music, and other arenas) always emphasizes sustained engagement at the highest level with deliberate practice (i.e., with feedback on specific goals, unending persistence). Thank you for this creative and impressive book, my friend Peter.

-Daniel Kirschenbaum, Ph.D., ABPP, Professor of Psychiatry & Behavioral Sciences, Northwestern University; former President, Division of Exercise and Sport Psychology, American Psychological Association

101 Finish Lines is a reflective, thought-provoking travel guide of marathons run around the world. However, hidden within is a contemplative handbook for the marathon of life. Filled with nuggets of wisdom, Dr. Nieman takes you on a soulful inner journey. Whether you are interested in his incredible streak of 101 marathons in some extraordinary places or are seeking some lessons to help guide your life, you will find strength, inspiration, and sage advice for crossing your own finish lines.

-David Irvine, author of *The Other Everest: Navigating The Pathway To Authentic Leadership*

101

FINISH
LINES

REFLECTIONS OF A PHYSICIAN DURING THE
QUEST TO CONQUER 100 MARATHONS

DR. PETER NIEMAN

BALBOA.PRESS
A DIVISION OF HAY HOUSE

Balboa Press books may be ordered through booksellers or by contacting:

Balboa Press
A Division of Hay House
1663 Liberty Drive
Bloomington, IN 47403
www.balboapress.com
844-682-1282

Print information available on the last page.

ISBN: 978-1-9822-6496-3 (sc)
ISBN: 978-1-9822-6495-6 (hc)
ISBN: 978-1-9822-6497-0 (e)

Library of Congress Control Number: 2021903984

Balboa Press rev. date: 04/26/2021

CONTENTS

INTRODUCTION

It was a warm, calm, peaceful Friday morning in June when I entered the south end of Central Park, wearing only shorts, a T-shirt, and well-worn running shoes.

I was in New York City to do a talk for a group of pediatricians interested in preventing burnout. One of my life-callings is to share knowledge particularly in the areas of personal wellness, and whenever I get to travel—*especially* to my favorite city, New York—it energizes me greatly. What this city represents speaks very loudly to me; even when some complain it is too busy and congested, being in Central Park, and connecting with nature there, always serves as a mental upgrade—an attainment of inner peace.

As a physician, passionate in helping others maintain wellness, I felt blessed to have given another talk on what wellness means and, perhaps more importantly, how to *sustain* it.

The theme of consistency dominates my being. To be able to sustain any behavior over many decades is to me a profound privilege. I aim to never take my many blessings for granted. I have observed over many years of running that life itself is really an exercise about setting priorities. What do we care about the most? Today, in Central Park, my priority was simple: be here now, *fully* in this very moment. At the center of my thought pattern was a deep sense that this is where I need to be right now.

> The theme of consistency dominates my being.

The talk the night before went well and I felt the run may have served as a reward —a moment where I got to play in an environment that has always meant so much to me during previous visits to New York City.

One of my favorite marathons is the New York City Marathon which usually takes place in November. It was seven years since I last ran in Central Park. Unlike the cool November air, this glorious June day was particularly warm.

My goal was to run around in this iconic park for a few hours and with clear blue skies above and the sun reflecting off the buildings along Central Park West, it did not take long to lose my sense of time and my sense of self. I was in the zone, a blissful peak state, within minutes, breathing in fresh morning air and intermittently monitoring my heart rate. Mindfulness teachers refer to this as a flow state. I was concentrating only on *one* single thing: being fully in the now…. soaking up all there was to soak up about the present. For a while I had absolutely no desire to be anywhere else.

I was fully absorbed in the moment and almost in a "heaven-like", "trance-like" consciousness, when I noticed in my peripheral vison, a robed man approaching me cautiously. I could tell by the dark orange color of the robe and his shaved head that he was a Buddhist monk. I slowed down. His face looked serene. The *moment* our eyes met I sensed a definite union between us. He felt like a brother. Instantly we felt joined. He radiated nothing but a deep inner peace and a healing quietness.

I have heard various people refer to vibes between humans as being good or bad—something that can be "picked up" instantly. In the radiant presence of my new friend, I felt *only* good energy and good vibes.

As we got closer, I noticed his big brown eyes peering down toward the beads he carried in one hand. He wanted to hand the beads over to me, but I could tell he did not speak any English. No words were needed though. I trusted him. We exchanged my cash for his beads and we respectfully bowed toward one another, holding our palms together, close to our hearts. The deep respect and the transcendence of varied backgrounds we felt were mutual.

I waved goodbye, treasuring in my heart the overflowing of a deep sense of love, joy. and peace while heading north toward the famous Central Park reservoir.

I still have the beads which I wear during some runs and on special occasions when I need a physical reminder to be kind and compassionate and that I am here on the planet to be truly helpful. We all are called to serve others. We are called to share our talents.

To this day, this brief interaction remains indelibly imprinted on my memory. It is one of literally thousands of memories related to my quest of finishing 100 marathons by age sixty.

In your hands you are holding a book filled with stories and life lessons I experienced. It is an honor to share them with you—from the same heart which kept me alive throughout the training and completion of 112 marathons at the time of the writing of the book.

I have one request before you read this book. Please do not compare yourself to me or others who "run" next to you on your own life's journey. This book is not about comparing or competing. It is about the celebration of our unique selves as humans while bringing out the best in others.

We are all unique. But it is also true that just like the monk who met me ever-so-briefly in New York City, we are human beings with basic similarities such as a desire to be peaceful inside and to find ways that will bring us happiness and purpose.

I passionately believe that every person has value and a unique destiny. May this book help you find clarity on your own purposeful path toward the end of your life.

There is no need to be a runner to get something from this book. I wrote it for one reason only: using stories and lessons birthed from my running experiences to help us reflect on ways we can move forward toward a finish line we have in mind—always on purpose.

In Hawaii, the word for moving forward is Imua. It refers to being resilient. There is a finish line many of us aspire to reach while we get to enjoy this ride on a rock, known as planet earth. We are going at an incredible speed through a vast and dark space. But one day there is a finish line.

That metaphorical finish line we aspire to reach may be:

- Physical, spiritual, or mental in nature. Or perhaps even a healthy balance of *all* three.

Like the Buddha, I cannot claim that what I am sharing will *definitely* move you forward. But I encourage you to try it on for size and see for yourself. Go ahead…take a bite and taste and see for yourself. Unless we experience anything personally, we never fully know.

I believe the author Ernest Hemmingway said, "In order to write about life, first you must live it." I have lived through 112 marathons thus far. What I wrote, is what I *lived*.

I welcome you on this "run" with me—even though you may be slumped on a couch or horizontal on a deck chair, next to a cool, clear, refreshing pool in Hawaii, or Mexico, or Florida during a winter break. Let us call it your virtual run.

I will take you to the tip of Africa, the Golden Gate Bridge in San Francisco, to sacred places in Hawaii, to a saloon somewhere remote in Alberta, to the Vietnam War Memorial in Washington D.C, to Canada's largest city, to the Canadian Rockies and into my own neighborhood.

The top two lessons or metaphors in life that running marathons have taught me are:

- Pacing oneself according to one's unique design is extremely crucial to sustain the distance and ultimately get to the finish line.
- Crowds along the way may encourage the runners, but without exception it is every runner who must do his or her own running. Crowds cannot do it on their behalf.

And so, it is with life. We learn along the way what pace works the best and we notice that the choices we make depend ultimately on us rather than circumstances or people in our lives.

Aversions may arise along the way, but contentment is possible. And as Santayana once wrote "There is no cure for birth and death, save to enjoy the interval."

This book is about the so-far-interval in my life—the observations and many illuminating lessons I gained in a quest to run over 100 marathons. By Grace I finished each race I started.

Thank you for being open to be a neighbor in my neighborhood by reading the pages of this book. Only read the ones you like the most. Read it at a pace that works for you. May it resonate with where you are at this time in your own "race" or season.

Peter Nieman

Canada, 2020

IN THE BEGINNING

While doing my undergraduate training in medical school, I was sitting in the peaceful and calm privacy of my room one Friday evening. It was dead quiet. I could almost hear my own heart beating.

Exam time was looming on the horizon, so naturally I had my mind focused on studying hard—medical school required quite a bit of commitment in terms of studying and getting through the times of testing to see if I would still be allowed to continue, or not. A great number of students dropped out at the early stages when the demands on their time and energy exceeded the dream to serve as a doctor.

I was deeply absorbed in reading a textbook when there was a sudden loud knock on my door. A fellow medical student, one of the fittest squash players I ever met, appeared in my line of vision.

It was my friend Maurice. I discovered long ago that all Maurice had to do was keep me running on the squash court until he could win a point with a killer shot... there was no way that I would ever outlast him! He was far, far too skilled to be beaten.

I can still to this day hear his enthusiastic voice boom in my direction. He called me "Pete". After almost shouting out "Pete!!" I heard these words: "I have entered us in a marathon tomorrow morning. There is *no f**cking way* I am going to allow you to drop out of this. Are you in or not? Don't be a chicken Pete!" I had no hope to keep up with him on the squash court, but what about doing a marathon? Perhaps I could beat him there?

My first thoughts were quite simple and logical. *You must be kidding me Maurice! There is no way I can run 26.2 miles just like that with no proper training….*

> In the distance, right next to the Atlantic Ocean, almost at the tip of Africa, I saw the majestic Table Mountain looming over Cape Town.

Well…to make a long story short, we did it. At first, we ran together and as the miles were "chewed up" underneath or sneakers, I could tell Maurice was getting a bit paler and paler by the minute while I was still feeling on top of the world. In the distance, right next to the Atlantic Ocean, almost at the tip of Africa, I saw the majestic Table Mountain looming over Cape Town. It was as if I were on top of that mountain for the next few hours looking down at all the troubles of the world. I was on top of everything— or so I thought.

I suppose it was my first experience of a runners high! I only discovered later in my running career that there is such a thing as an endorphin rush which makes your brain feel invincible.

In those days when one did a marathon you had to supply your own support for liquids and food. So I had another medical student drive my old beat-up lily-white Volkswagen Beatle, encountering me every 3 miles or so with something to keep my body from running dry or hitting the empty zone. Insufficient calories left in the tank is not an unfamiliar event for marathoners. It is known as "hitting the wall."

As the race unfolded, this friend, called Joe, became part of my team. It became the two of us versus the rest of the world! In the beginning Joe was there to merely drive my car and provide my sustenance, but as we progressed, the bond between us grew stronger and stronger. It was as if Joe now had some skin in the game, even though he did not have to slog away in the heat and wind, covering a marathon distance.

With only a few miles left, Joe waved me goodbye. I thought that was it. I was now going to be alone. But as a I rounded the corner before the finish line…there was Joe, running the last few hundred yards with me, beaming a proud smile as our eyes met and telling me that Maurice was tuckered out and puking all over the place a few miles behind us. Joe's enthusiastic pat on my shoulder almost knocked me right over like a bowling pin. I could hardly propel my body to the finish line, which was only a few hundred yards ahead.

Finally, I outlasted my friend Maurice! But in this sport, most marathoners are like comrades and when *one* hurts, we all feel for that person! Compassion means to suffer with. After completing my marathon, I was ready to suffer with Maurice. A few minutes later, Joe and I went back on the course to support our buddy. Maurice liked that a lot….

The next day with amused smiles on our faces, Maurice and I looked at our bruised toes and chaffed skin. It was my crazy friend's idea to take on a marathon with the *only* preparation being a game of squash which we both were good at. But to this day when I am asked "What got you into running?" I always tell this story, knowing that:

- **The tallest trees in a forest once began as a small seed. Uncertain of how things may end, we still must plant a seed.**

PLACES

I feel blessed to have literally travelled all over
the planet to run over 100 marathons.

Here are some stories about places which really
stirred my spirit, soul, and body.

**Wheresoever you go, go with all your heart.
—Confucius**

BOURBON STREET AT DAWN

New Orleans is one of my favorite cities to visit. Usually, I am there to attend conferences. I was told that the Convention Center is one of the biggest in North America. Hearing it is not the same as experiencing it. There is enough space in the center to accommodate the fields and courts for all the games in the NFL and NBA on one weekend to be held simultaneously.

Not so long ago I started my day in New Orleans the way I start all my days—a morning run at sunrise. The poem by the famous Indian Dramatist, Kalidasa, came to mind when I looked toward the east where the sun was about to rise in a few minutes.

*SALUTATION TO THE DAWN**

> *Look to this day!*
> *For it is life, the very life of life.*
> *In its brief course*
> *Lie all the verities and realities of your existence.*
> *Look well therefore to this day!*
> *Such is the salutation to the dawn*

Just before dawn I stepped into the warm, humid morning air. It was still semi-dark, but the skies toward the east were slowly getting brighter and brighter by the minute. I headed to one of the main attractions in the Emerald City—Bourbon Street.

---

* For a complete version of this poem, see https://www.jtdschool.com/list-detail?pk=13849

Not sure what to expect at six in the morning, I rounded the corner and saw Bourbon Street littered by papers, sticky drinks still to be washed off the cobblestoned-streets and discarded beads torn in half. Some bars were still open. Even at dawn, notes of the jazz music echoed through an almost deserted, but littered street.

I felt privileged to enjoy my body's vitality. Aware of the gift of another new dawn, I observed all the famous tourist sights of New Orleans. My mind wandered when suddenly one person stood out… a drunk staggering toward me. As I got closer, I could see he was impressed by me— this crazy runner out so early in the day. As I passed him, he high fived me and shouted, "YES!" The good times were indeed rolling at six A.M. He experienced a beverage high and I experienced a runner's high.

I had no doubt in my mind that my friend was happy—for a moment at least, thanks to his partying until dawn. But would he still be happy at noon? That was not for me to judge.

Who knows? But this I know for sure: We all get to decide what works and what does not work. Our priorities are ours to choose. All throughout our days we face pivotal forks in the road, trade-offs, decisions which determine our destiny.

As a doctor over the past 40 years, I have observed some common patterns. The happiest people are those who have found the perfect sweet spot, a deep awareness, and a profound sense of balance in four key areas of simplified living: movement, rest, fueling and attitude.

I came up with an acronym of NEST when I think of the four wheels of wellness: Nutrition, Exercise, Sleep, and Thoughts.

I feel blessed to be able to run every day and move my body at a pace that suits my age and energy. I have seen the results of burnout because of a pace that is not sustainable. Rest matters a great deal and how we sleep, relax, meditate, and recover makes all the difference between one finish line or 101 finish lines.

Fueling our bodies with natural foods, non-refined and non-processed, and in moderate amounts just seems so simple and yet few people do it. They fuel for pleasure rather than energy. It is a mystery to me that when we know the things we know, we often do the opposite; doing the unhealthy things we do, almost mindlessly at times. Even when physical aspects of healthy living predominate the conversations we have with our doctors, we often forget the ace in our deck of cards—-the card that trumps all others; our attitude. The way we choose our thoughts every second of every day.

Preachers are not quoted that often these days in our modern secular culture, but Chuck Swindoll, a veteran preacher of almost 50 years, once said that attitude is 90 % of our success. I have seen him quoted at least 100 times in various articles and books over the years.

> *The longer I live the more I realize the impact of attitude on life. Attitude, to me, is more important than the past, than education, than money, than circumstances, than failures, than successes, than what other people think, say, or do.*
>
> *It is more important than appearance, giftedness, or skill. It will make or break a company.... a church.... a home. The remarkable thing is we have a choice every day regarding the attitude we embrace for that day.*
>
> *We cannot change our past. We cannot change the fact that many people will act in a certain way. We cannot change the inevitable.*
>
> *The only thing we can do is play the one string we have, and that is our attitude.... I am convinced that life is 10% what happens to me and 90% how I react to it. And so it is with you.... we are in charge of our attitudes.*

- **The difference between one and 101 finish lines comes down to one word: attitude....be in charge of cultivating a healthy attitude.**

BALD OPEN PRAIRIES

I was training for my next marathon—Las Vegas to be precise. Vegas is a place where I first qualified for a Boston marathon, mostly because of a downhill course! I may not be the fastest runner in my age group, but at least I am one of the most persistent ones. When I see a downhill course, I get excited—even *more* so as I age.

I thought of my past visits to Vegas and reminded myself that gambling is fun, but more so when one wins. I was determined to "win" by training properly for once, rather than run yet another marathon, hoping that my muscle-memory would get me to the finish line in a reasonable time.

While on holiday somewhere on the prairies of Saskatchewan, I found myself surrounded by wheat fields stretching as far as the eye could see. The fields were pulsating slowly and rhythmically in the gentle breezes sweeping across the prairies. The air was warm and refreshing and the pleasant contrast with my runs in minus 40C wind chills was totally in sync with my preferences.

There is a joke about a farmer who went to visit the beautiful Canadian Rockies. When asked what he thought of the tall mountains I often call "The Alps without a jet lag", he responded, "These mountains sure are pretty, but they spoil my view."

> A typical hardy Canadian also once observed that there is no such a thing as cold weather....one just has to dress appropriately for it.

The same farmer, a typical hardy Canadian, also once observed that there is no such a thing as cold weather....one just has to dress appropriately for it. In the middle of winter in Canada I see few runners got that message. Instead, they are on treadmills, inside.

But today it was warm and sunny. I had a perfect view for miles and looking up I saw nothing but deep, blue skies, big and wide, extending far above the wheat fields. Below the living skies were these seemingly endless fields of pale-colored wheat extending to the farthest edges of the horizon.

Butterflies danced and floated closer to my path on a dirt road. In one hour of running, I encountered only two vehicles... probably farmers on their way to town to get some supplies. Both delivered friendly waves in my direction. I looked down at my fitness tracker, sure of its GPS accuracy.

A few years ago, I found myself in the canyons of skyscrapers in Chicago, running the same 26.2 miles the famous Oprah Winfrey ran. Given the magnitude of the concrete jungle, my GPS was way off. The tall buildings blocked the satellite signal to my wrist. Out on the prairie, with nothing taller than a granary in site, the signal was clear and accurate.

I learned a valuable lesson. Fitness trackers are helpful, but not always accurate.

Since my Chicago marathon, and during my prairie run under wide open, living skies, getting ready for Las Vegas, I reminded myself of the words spoken by former President Ronald Reagan: "Trust, but verify."

- **Be free and float like a butterfly while remaining open to whatever the present may bring. Nevertheless, trust but verify.**

TWO OCEANS

I have only done one ultra-marathon and I plan to keep it that way. Marathons that last only 26.2 miles suit me simply fine. Anything longer is too long.

As a kid I grew up in South Africa in a place called Durban. Imagine the heat and humidity of Florida. Imagine all kinds of snakes, cockroaches, and insects. Imagine pristine beaches with miles and miles of sandy shores welcoming waves rolling in from the mighty deep blue Indian Ocean.

The Comrades Marathon takes place between Durban and Pietermaritzburg. It is seen by many as the granddaddy of all ultra-marathons. I still remember as a child, growing up in Durban, our family glued to the radio at the start of the Comrades. In those days there were no TV's in South Africa. We tuned in to the radio at the start of the race and heard the announcer telling the runners to "Line up and get ready…Set…and… GO!"

The go part was marked by the sound of a rooster at dawn, just when the sun almost cleared the horizon. That was when runners from all over the planet started their almost 96 kilometers journey; one year uphill to the end at a place called Pietermaritzburg and the other year a downhill course and the same distance to Durban, the port city where I grew up. Each year it alternated, but the distance was always the same—a grueling 96 kilometers.

It was not for me. I prefer marathons…way shorter than 96 kilometers and easier to do. But I did what many Canadians do so well: I compromised. I flew to Cape Town and ran a shorter ultra-marathon at the tip of

Africa known as "the world's most beautiful marathon", the Two Oceans Marathon.

There I was early one morning in one of the most beautiful cities in the Southern Hemisphere, about to do something I had never done before— run *more* than 26.2 miles. Imagine a five A.M. start in one of the world's most scenic environments.

As I type these words, I am enjoying a fine South African wine by the same name—Two Oceans. There is something special about that name. Africa is big, and oceans are big…so it is a big deal when the Atlantic and Indian Oceans meet.

Around the time of this marathon the planet was fretting as we transitioned from the year 1999 to 2000. The fear was that the world would fall apart at the seams. I was worried that I would fall apart somewhere along the long, tedious, hilly course.

Instead of focusing on fears I focused on the ocean next to me. I have always been attracted to life next to the ocean. According to researchers, known as echotherapists—scientists who study how our brain and our environment interact—we do have in all of us what is called a Blue Mind.

In a book with that title, Wallace J. Nichols wrote that our brain changes to a healthy structure when we find ourselves close to a body of water, be it the ocean, lakes, or rivers. By scanning human brains, using a functional MRI scanner, researchers have shown what is called neuroplasticity—meaning the brain can literally alter its physical and physiological state when we spend enough time next to water.

I am sure my brain was also altered by running such a long distance! Much to my relief, I managed to finish. There I was under African skies after crossing the finish line with a "mere" 56 kilometers behind me— 14 kilometers longer than a standard marathon. I was flat on my back supported by soft green grass, looking up at the vast blue skies. Not a single cloud was seen and as I closed my eyes, I immediately knew this to be true:

- **Run only a distance that resonates with your own preferences. Never compete or compare, but instead be who you are and make sure you finish strong.**

LAST CHANCE SALOON

I have noticed how stories generated by my quest to complete 100 marathons have led others to respond with *their* stories and one that particularly resonated was the story I heard on the patio of the Last Chance Saloon. It took place at the start of a memorable vacation where I had plans to use the extra time to relax, but also to train for another marathon.

My wife and I headed off east, and in our rear view mirror the mighty Rockies became smaller and smaller. In an upgraded new rental car, we were heading toward the wide-open Canadian Prairies. But before we got there, we found ourselves in a saloon in Southern Alberta. It is called Last Chance Saloon and dates to 1913 when coal mines were still thriving. Bullet holes can still be seen in the walls of this quaint place.

My run in Central Park —the story about the Buddhist monk— triggered a conversation with a friendly, outgoing waitress. She noticed the Buddhist beads on my right wrist. I told her the story you may have read at the start of this book.

As I said in the introduction, some runs are marked by peak states where everything just ends up in an extended slow motion of pure bliss and joy. I shared with her how this monk smiled and offered me a string of beads—18 beads. Each bead probably representing something meaningful.

> There seems to be something special about the number 18.

There seems to be something special about the number 18. In the Tao Tradition, 18 represents something important; in the Jewish tradition the number is deeply meaningful. Golfers will tell us that 18 holes mean something special too!

The waitress at the Last Chance Saloon shared *her* Buddhist monk story in return.

Apparently, they had a mysterious and lonely Zen monk visit them; bright orange robes gave away his identity and calling. He did not speak English. She wanted her picture taken with him. She probably had never seen a monk in this remote saloon in the middle of almost-nowhere in Alberta, Canada.

After the picture was captured for posterity, she came close to him and, very spontaneously, but sincerely, hugged him. This was a big mistake. The waitress went on to explain to me that, "It set off quite a commotion and led to the monk's immediate departure."

"Never touch the monk" she learned despite her innocent and sincere motives. She said she apologized and promised to never do it again. But the monk left anyway. He was quite upset I was told.

And so, my time in Central Park caused a conversation—as do many other marathon stories.

Later that day as I allowed my head to drop on my pillow, I reminded myself that all humans really have their own stories. It is mostly stories about two goals; two great desires. These stories may vary but…

- **Two universal human needs are the needs to be happy and to be free of suffering. Let us always remember *that* whenever we encounter any stranger.**

THE BRIDGE

It was a stunningly beautiful morning. I was on a roll. I felt like Forest Gump in that I could just run and run with no desire to stop. But I stopped. You will soon see why.

Through my veins flowed a *deep* inner state of joy as I heard my footsteps and the footsteps of thousands of other runners strike the surface of the Golden Gate Bridge. We were heading south, having just completed the northern part of this race, which meandered just outside Sausalito. We were heading back to Golden Gate Park, and after that, the Haight-Ashbury district and ultimately to the finish line along the Embarcadero.

I was in the middle of this long parade of colorful human beings on an iconic bridge. People from all over the planet with one goal in mind: to cross the finish line and bask in the accomplishment of enduring and conquering all kinds of physical and emotional challenges.

I had no reason to stop. But I could not help it. I stopped. There was no way I was going to merely flash by what I saw. A few yards ahead of me, I saw a handsome guy on his knees, looking up at the love of his life, a beautiful, slim, tall, healthy, young blond lady with a long ponytail. Both were doing the same marathon I was enjoying so much at the time.

I discovered it was *the time* he elected to propose and ask her "Will you marry me?" The location was stunning. To my left was the San Francisco Bay and the island of Alcatraz. To my right I noticed the deep, and today, the unusually calm Pacific stretching far toward the edge of the horizon.

She beamed one of the widest smiles I have ever seen. I saw her lily-white teeth only briefly before she covered her mouth. In a huge moment of surprise and disbelief, she passionately shrieked out loudly "I do…I DO!"

I doubt this couple noticed the natural beauty surrounding them at that moment; they probably only noticed each other's eyes. But no doubt, later as they continued the race together, they probably soaked in what had just happened and amplified their joy by observing the beautiful scenery.

I heard a few Ooooh's and Aaaah's from other runners who also saw what I just saw.

Suddenly it hit me: we all are the same. We all want to love and be loved. What was different about this handsome prince is that he chose an unusual time to ask his best friend to marry him.

I was reminded of this insight:

- **When you plan special moments, make sure you do it in style. Not only will it be easier to remember for a long time; you may also bring joy to others.**

DIP OR DIVE?

It was a warm summer's day. As usual I got my daily inspirational e-mails and quotes that morning.

As a writer, I am always scanning my world for new ideas - like a photographer scanning the environment for another unique and gripping picture. As soon as I have a moment, I record these ideas with my favorite fountain pen in a journal. Here is an example of a quote by Sam Keen which I received that day:

- "Deep summer is when laziness finds respectability."

I was keen to be lazy after completing the hilly and hot San Francisco marathon and my dear wife did what she does so well: she found a fine restaurant for us, located right next to the Pacific, and a few blocks west of Golden Gate Park.

The great discovery from doing these things, not half-heartedly, but fully committed (I run about four marathons a year) is that it is a metaphor for life. When I finish a marathon, I am usually exhausted. It sucks plenty of energy out of all of us. The Kenyans may be an exception; but then again... these humans are amazing runners from Africa who glide, seemingly effortlessly, as soon as they run. They were born to run. To watch them on TV is no match for witnessing their grace in person.

But after each of the past 112 marathons I always recovered. Life may hand you a lemon and you reframe it by making lemonade. As an athlete I know for sure that fatigue is followed by new fuel if one skillfully gets re-plugged in properly; the right rest, the right food, and the right attitude.

Setbacks may drain you dry. You are exhausted by the daily struggles; the ups and downs of life; often made worse by poor health, unsatisfactory relationships, and lack of sufficient finances. But know this: *just make it to the finish line and recovery is possible.*

After getting my energy back after running this specific marathon, a very scenic but hilly marathon, I gingerly and slowly got into an Uber with my wife. We headed west from our downtown hotel. The Pacific coast was waiting for us.

Soon after the Uber driver waved us goodbye, I dipped my feet in the ice-cold Pacific Ocean. As I did that, I recalled the words of Dennis Wilson of the Beach Boys who once said, "On the beach, you can live in bliss."

I was in a state of bliss, having completed another tough marathon where the steep hills make such an experience extra special. When I do that particular race - and I have done it almost a dozen times - I focus on the scenery and forget to look at my fitness tracker which tells me my time, distance and speed. Nobody chooses a hilly race to run a personal best. Checking one's heart rate is futile. There is no point. The point shifts to *just finish this sucker and pretend you feel good.*

During the absolute peak of my beach moment, I could not care less about Martin Seligman PhD, the guru who came up with the idea of positive psychology. Seligman once wrote that, "I actually detest the word happiness, which is so overused that it has become almost meaningless."

I was simply happy and amazingly content. There was no other place I would rather be at that moment. I was smelling the ocean air, tasting salt on my lips, listening to the waves rolling toward the shore and noticing a patch of cool mist heading toward the beach. San Francisco can be "weird" and wild in the summers at times. It can be cool, due to the fog which drifts in from the Pacific and blocks out the sun.

Mark Twain was credited with the saying that, "The coldest winter I ever spent was a summer in San Francisco."

Physically all the above were true, but what was also true is that mentally we all get to choose how we dip ourselves into a cause we care about. Mental fog tends to dim finish lines.

The physical aspects of running are easy to do and understand. The mental and spiritual aspects I believe, take far more effort of digging deeper. Some have called this digging deeper one of the longest journeys, even though it is only 12 inches. The distance between the head (logic) and the heart (soul and spirit) may be 12 inches, but it takes a warrior and hero's attitude to travel that distance.

Imagine a teacher who is happily married. Her world fell apart when her beloved husband failed in his efforts to deal with an addiction. Today she tells of how many women must face what she calls the 4D's (death, divorce, debt and disability).

What was the pivot for her? How did she overcome this amazing test of her resilience? Her tool may not be for all, but she found it worked for her: she discovered a regular practice of cultivating mindfulness every morning.

Mindfulness has been popularized by Dan Harris, host of the Podcast *Ten Percent Happier*. In essence, mindfulness meditation allows us to be fully present and to really feel our feelings without being intimidated by them. We put an end to being yanked around by thoughts.

So often I am reminded when I run, of feeling every step along the way. It is impossible to literally feel each step, but at least when we are mindful more often, we get better at being fully present.

Cultivating physical fitness has been fun for me over the past three decades, but it was only recently that I discovered the bliss of cultivating mindfulness. It is for me the ability just to be where I am; fully present, with no need to fix anything or judge anyone.

Mindfulness provided a deep sense of satisfactoriness; a sense of here I am now, fully aware of what is, grateful to be alive, sucking in ocean air deep down into the bottom of my lungs, feeling sand underneath my feet, and overflowing in a state of bliss.

Even when some of the most respected gurus on the planet try to convince us that they detest the word "happiness", I experienced it fully by not merely dipping, but by diving deeper.

Dipping is a more-or-less approach; diving is not half-hearted - it is all in. I tell my friends to be all in. I often go on to ask them "How can your heart be on fire when your wood is wet?"

One of the areas of my life where I remained fully committed is the habit of daily exercise - like daily sleeping and daily eating. It is all about commitment to a plan that I sometimes call: WWFU.

Whatever works for you.

I am often reminded to really be present; to really feel and to absorb what is happening right here and right now.

- **Now is the time to decide how deep you want to dive and lean into what matters the most to you. Once you know, then commit to it fully.**

DROUGHT

One morning, while in Sacramento, I ran with my wife. She loves roses.

We were about five minutes away from our hotel and encountered a famous rose garden not far from where Ronald Reagan and Arnold Schwarzenegger occupied the Governor's office in the State Capital.

The roses were the only fortunate "creatures" to get access to water that morning. Green lawns became white and dry. There was a terrible drought in California. Things were bad. Water restrictions applied to everything in the park except the roses.

There is a saying that it's always five o'clock somewhere. I say, good for that kind of happiness as long as it is not out of control. But it is also true that at anytime somewhere on the planet there is a drought.

Marriages have droughts; friendships have droughts; jobs and the economy experience droughts. Seasons come and seasons go in this imperfect world where impermanence is as true as the rising of the morning sun.

Allow me to tell you about a drought that taught me great lessons. This drought ends with a yoga class but began with severe back ache.

A few years ago, I almost ended my running streak which started on December 16, 2009. For no clear reason, my back, which never ever bothered me before, acted up. Physiotherapists who previously helped me, failed greatly this time. One even told me to stop running. Of course, I deleted that pop-up "warning", masquerading as friendly advice, as quickly

17

as possible. Even though well-meaning, that was not going to work for me. It was simply non-negotiable.

I continued to run through a drought; no marathons, no races, and only short distance runs.

Then synchronistically, I ended up in a Saturday morning class at a yoga studio, a stone's throw from my home. This class, taught by my teacher Travis, is known as a yoga class for stiff old men. I should mention that Travis has a great sense of humor which adds to the healing. He always warns us old men that we must be ready to go into the King of all Poses at any time. He also asks us to hang on to some poses a bit longer to practice for the day the students in our class for stiff men will be posing for a calendar! (The calendar part probably will happen only *after* satan skates to work on ice.)

Yoga made all the difference. I returned to training and competing very soon after experiencing yoga's healing energies and simultaneously discovered the mental joys of this new practice and a more mindful way of living. In fact, because of yoga, I now set an intention before every activity. Even in between patients I set intentions such as "May I be *truly* helpful and serve with wisdom and compassion."

Droughts pass, but their lessons stay if we choose to remain open and willing to learn. What I learned from my painful "drought" was simply this:

- **Don't listen only to experts; also listen to your own heart or gut-instinct. Stay patient in drought seasons because that which will arise, also will pass at some point.**

THE SMELL

One of my favorite vacation spots on the whole planet is Cabo San Lucas, Mexico. I have been there at least a dozen times and not *once* did it rain on me. There were clouds at the start of one day, but they had no chance to last—the heat of the sun close to the Equator rapidly burned them off; complete evaporation did not take long.

The first time I ever did a two-hour morning run in the Cabo San Lucas region was memorable for two reasons—I underestimated the heat even very early in the day and I ended up being grateful for my nose.

I had to rehydrate rapidly following a very hot and humid half marathon run under Mexican skies. As I sat in the shade of our balcony, it occurred to me that the logical thing to do would be to simply open a Mexican-made beer, enjoying every small sip, while admiring sun worshipers, jet ski enthusiasts, para-sailing fanatics, and hearing the happy sounds of birds hopping around, waiting for breadcrumbs to be consumed with zeal.

I can still see and feel the dew forming on the outside of the beer bottle as it transitioned from the fridge to a warmer environment.

A short while after my balcony time I became restless and entered the spa. It is a peaceful place where one can get pampered with all manner of soothing treatments. The air in the reception area was filled with a fragrance I had never experienced in the past. It is hard to properly describe but allow me to simply say it was a fragrance I wanted to take back to Canada with me.

And I did!

I discovered I was not the only one to be impressed by the smell. Apparently other visitors were impacted too. The company who runs the spa wisely made a spray which is available for purchase.

My considerate wife knows how much I enjoy this fragrance and, as a doctor, she also knows that smells can take us back to pleasant memories. Occasionally when we feel "home sick" for our home away from home, she sprays the fragrance in our bathroom. How our memories are triggered by smells is a topic worth reading more about in a scientific journal.

But maybe you would rather relax than engage in research, so may I invite you to:

- **Use your sense of smell to take you back, even for a brief moment, to a smell which brings alive pleasant memories in an instant.**

NO RUNNING ALLOWED

One of my favorite cities to visit is Washington D.C. I have explored the core of this globally influential city mostly on foot: completely unplanned and unprepared.

My first ever visit was with my wife and ten-year-old daughter after a nightmare flight from Canada via Minneapolis. Leaving Canada was easy, but it was a good thing we did not know what lay ahead. As soon as we landed in Minneapolis and looked for the gate to our connecting flight to DC, we saw that the flight was cancelled due to weather. I looked at the clear blue skies outside the Minneapolis airport. That was the last time I would see the sun for a few days.

We were redirected to Philadelphia, and that was it. From there we were on our own. As far as plane "rides" go, this was the end of the line; the final stop.

A rental car transported us down the main highway to DC. But it was not that simple. The windshield wipers could not keep up with the downpour. Ambulances flashed by us to rescue stranded cars in ditches. It took what felt like forever to make it to DC a few hours after midnight.

Being a creature of habit, I rose at the usual time of six A.M. and headed out to run, not knowing which direction was east (my usual clue is to look at where the sky shines the brightest before dawn, but today there was nothing but pouring, relentless, rain). The ominous skies had the same morbid and uniform deep grey color. A half-hour later I rounded a corner and spotted the White House where I paused and wondered about some of the historic moments which unfolded behind those walls.

I continued my run with no idea where I was heading and then turned another corner where I discovered the Vietnam War Memorial. As I approached the memorial, I noted a figure in a dark uniform. Assuming he was a guard or a military servant I slowed down. That was a good thing.

With a booming voice I was told, "Sir, excuse me. No running is allowed here."

I never knew this, but one can run just about anywhere in the USA except one place: the Vietnam War Memorial. It makes sense that one has to show respect to the departed. I walked…respectfully wondering about the price of freedom, the need for wars and the meaning of death and dying.

That memorable day in D.C. I learned this useful lesson:

- **There are times when one learns the most by exploring new opportunities with curiosity.**

THE SPRAYER

One of my favorite activities is to run with a buddy. Not all buddies are the same.

If diamonds are a girl's best friend, how come man ended up with a dog?

Seriously...Sage, a beautiful Black Labrador dog I once had the honor to run with, now long departed, is still with me when I run. I carry her in my heart. Unexpectedly and out of the blue, destiny took her away from me.

Osteosarcoma is known to cause silent harm and by the time the lump on her knee was discovered it was too late. The cancer spread all over her beautiful body. Her outside consisted of a shiny coat, just like her curious eyes, always shiny except when they were sad, as she too knew before she transitioned that her life was over. Meanwhile her inside was ravaged by destructive cancer cells determined to end her life.

My best buddy, my wife, is still with me on some runs. And for that I am deeply grateful.

There is one place where she pretty much always joins me. It is in the Canadian Rockies, in a place called Canmore. It has become my go-to spot to cultivate deep inner peace in nature. It is a consistent oasis of new energy. This place is also a bit like a photogenic women - even if you try your best, it is *impossible* to take a bad picture.

One can point one's camera in any direction and end up with a photo that resonates with almost 100% of people who see it on social media.

During a recent run something unusual happened. It was warm for a change!

I often remind myself that the capital C in Canada stands for *capital* cold. C also is for *constantly* cold. Some Canadians are like polar bears and Huskies - they like it cold. Take them to anywhere with palm trees and ocean breezes and they complain it is too hot!

But that day in the Rockies it was hot. How hot? Hot enough for Corinne to stand under a lawn sprinkler by our condo after we completed a one hour run together in the calm and undisturbed nature of Canmore, close to 4,200 feet above sea level.

I posted the photo of her doing that and as I close my eyes, I still see my beautiful wife by a sprinkler with the bright morning sun lighting up her shiny blond hair. I posted the photo on Facebook.

In case you think I am biased about her beauty, it was one of the most liked pictures ever posted on my Facebook feed, but then again, my posts are not as much for others as they are to remind myself that:

- **After you put in the effort, take time to relax. Savor every moment with a loved one, if possible**

THE FALL

It was a perfect sunny morning in January on Martin Luther King Day in Houston—one day after the Houston marathon. Since I run every day, even the very next day after a marathon, I went out for a slower than usual morning run. It took me close to the major league baseball park, home of the World Champion Houston Astros.

A short while later I saw stars in the Lone Star State.

I tripped on a piece of cement and saw my spectacular trajectory toward the sidewalk in slow motion. I landed with a thud and tried to rise. I was unable to get up. *Did I break something?* I thought.

People were already lined up for the start of the parade close to the stadium. A concerned lady came running toward me and asked, "Are you ok?" Bravely, and yet somewhat tentatively, I answered "yes". However, to cover the 1,000 meters back to my hotel took me almost one hour. I later discovered I had torn a muscle in my inner thigh. I ended up black and blue from my butt to the bottom of my foot a few days later.

Did my streak end? Not at all.

I should have known better as a doctor, but with a determined mind and tender muscles - under the influence of panikillers-I continued the next day and the next and the next …. albeit very slowly.

Things happen along the way. That is why I always try to remember adding these words after a sentence about my future: "God willing". Anything can happen at any time.

Before I go deeper into "God-willing" please allow me to make a detour. Stick with me please.

I always thought I controlled outcomes. It is easy to believe that when life works out and delivers at your doorstep what you believe and expect. I used to believe that throwing the dice was not good enough. We had to visualize and affirm the outcome before it landed. After all it is all up to us and a positive attitude which, supposedly, attracts both good and bad. But I now know we only throw the dice; we have zero control how it lands.

> But what if you don't believe in God?

That day in Houston, I picked up a metaphorical dice and saw a six in my mind, but the dice landed with an "unwanted" one - quite far from the desired six I was supposed to attract.

But what if you don't believe in God? What if you believe in an "Unseen Force"? What if you are like Thomas Edison and call God an "Infinite Intelligence"? What if you replace "God" with "The Universe"?

What if…

I don't have the answer. I really don't. These questions are far too deep for me.

In the now famous book, *The Secret*, we were told to use visualizations and affirmation to attract a six instead of a one. Don't we all desire sixes after all? So, I trusted a Higher Power to make my paths smooth. The longer I live, the less attractive I find the so-called Law of Attraction.

But I do know, for me, I feel better when I admit that I am not always able to see into the future…so I stand by my story of "God-Willing".

- **It is not a matter of whether things will happen along the way; they will. It's a matter of when. When that moment arrives … what is your plan? Mine is to never quit.**

SIMON IN AFRICA

I grew up in Africa. No…I did not have a farm in Africa as Meryl Streep said in the movie. But I grew up there, so I know a little bit about Africa. Many South Africans are serious runners and when one visits that country it is easy to see why that is so. It is a sport which does not require much equipment or money. The perpetual sunshine makes going outside very easy.

Recently on a run where I intentionally switched on my iPod right at the start, I heard some sounds from Africa. When I run, I love the rhythms of running accompanied by rhythms of music.

And who better to address the rhythm of music than Paul Simon? In his album "GRACELAND" inspired by African music, Simon takes me back to my childhood in sunny Africa.

> I believe every human being is born to deliver cargo - a gift unique to them.

I believe every human being is born to deliver cargo - a gift unique to them.

Africans have an amazing skill to harmonize with absolutely zero other influences - they just do it. All on their own. No instruments. They make it look so easy. Like the Kenyan who at the time of this writing became the first human to run a sub two hour marathon in Vienna; he did it seamlessly and effortlessly. Almost as if born to do just that.

My wife saw the video of this runner on a quest - her jaw was wide open when she noticed his energy *after* he crossed the finish line with no agony on his face at all and no sweat streaming down the rest of his lean body. Many Africans deliver their cargo seamlessly.

On a very diverse planet, it makes sense to not compete, but rather to:

- **Know the customized cargo you are designed to deliver and do it with wisdom and compassion.**

FREQUENT FLYER

Due to my work as a doctor, a coach, and an author in addition to doing marathons all over the planet, I have discovered that uncertainty is certain.

Frequent flying has taught me much, but whenever I head to an airport, I remind myself to be comfortable with uncertainty.

One just never knows how long the line ups will be, how the weather may change, which airline will experience computer issues, which planes will have last minute mechanical issues, when staff may decide to walk off the job, which selfish person will butt into a waiting area for boarding early, if you will be stuck in a small seat where the chair cannot recline, or if *your* overhead light is the *only* light in the whole plane which does not work.

One can count the above frustrations or count the humor which also unfolds occasionally.

During a recent trip I flew in a smaller jet—the ones made in Quebec… also known as regional jets. I call these little Canadian-made jets "Barbie jets" or "puddle jumpers". They seem to be used more often these days and they fly way farther than just regionally. I have an aversion to these dinky, cramped and frustratingly small planes.

On this flight there were only two flight attendants - one male and the other female. The latter made the announcements, and all went well until she caused a wave of giggling through the cramped cabin when she announced, "And in the front of the plane we have Joe, my former husband."

I have never heard such an announcement before, and I suspect I was not the only one to enquire later when we disembarked if that were true. It was not.

They were never married; they were just fellow crew members there to serve the cabin with excellent care and humor. The clue should have been that they looked *way* too comfortable in each other's company, working hard together and smiling far more than most former spouses do. (I know for some divorced couples they are best friends afterwards, but that is the exception rather than the rule.)

> Airline crews hide by plants in the Chicago airport.

Because Chicago is such a huge hub, I have spent almost one year of my life there, waiting for connections or getting there early because the line ups are so long. It is easy to miss a flight when one forgets to plan. A few years ago, I discovered where airline crew tend to hide from the hustle and bustle at ORD.

They "hide" by plants. It's a very peaceful area.

Surrounded by the steady trickle of water and the bright lights shining on an indoor aeroponic garden, on any given day, one can find pilots and flight attendants kicking back a bit, soaking in some peace and quiet in a very crowded airport known as one of the world's busiest connecting hubs. The area is known as an "Urban Garden".

Check it out next time you have a bit of extra time at ORD.

- **Peace in the middle of uncertainty is possible, but like a garden, inner peace needs to be consciously and consistently cultivated.**

THE RUNWAY

I live in a city which, at the time of this writing, has one of the world's longest runways. In fact, I once ran on this runway without getting arrested for trespassing.

It was a bright sunny morning and less than a few hundred runners boarded a yellow school bus in an airport parking lot. The bus was our transportation to the runway. Security was very tight. I felt like we were being smuggled through secretly to get to what was supposed to be a one-time only event.

We lined up at exactly the halfway mark of this long stretch of concrete. Two long lines of lights used by pilots of big jetliners during landings and take offs marked the edges of this brand-new runway. Huge numbers dotted the distances at various points, so pilots knew where they were along this vast strip which ran off into the distance.

It was an exclusive event organized by a well known Canadian store which specializes in the sale of superb quality running gear. They did this to raise money for charity and it was merely one week before the official opening of the runway.

Some celebrities could run this event for free and one even started to spontaneously talk to me - reaffirming my strong belief that all humans have a lot in common and even celebrities need to sleep. Even the most influential ones must stand on one leg when they put on their pants.

We all are monkeys really. We share very basic common needs and behaviors, but then there are times to be monkeys with tuxedos. It is when we take on roles of leaders, professionals, or celebrities. We forget the basics and pretend to be more sophisticated than we really are.

We first ran south, then all the way to the northern end and back to where we started at the half way mark of this amazing runway. Ten kilometers of sheer excitement, knowing that it would be our one and only time to be on the runway where our running shoes, unlike the rubber from jet wheels, would not leave a single mark.

The next time for all of us on this runway would be when we would find ourselves seated inside a plane, looking down with fond memories of having had the honor to run on it once in our lifetimes.

Since then, every time I pass the spot where the race started - looking down from my seat at the runway below... the words of the race announcer that day echo in my ears: *"You better enjoy today - really, really enjoy it, because next time you are on this runway, you will either be in a plane or arrested."*

- **Some opportunities indeed are once-in-a lifetime. Grab them while you can.**

FLIGHT PATHS

En route to a marathon I once had to make a connection via Denver. It is by far the most modern airport and has stood the test of time by still functioning as it should over at least two decades, without the need to disrupt the lives of passengers by endlessly renovating the terminals year after year after year. There are no signs apologizing for messes. The point of these signs is to remind us to be glad for all the improvements which supposedly will serve us better in the days to come.

Denver is a connection I try to avoid if possible—the weather in that area can be strange: winds coming off the Rockies and unexpected blizzards that paralyze flights and cause major delays and detours. I once watched a movie *Under the Tuscan sun,* sitting for hours in the same place on a tarmac, waiting for other planes to get de-iced. Once again, the staff at Denver got caught by surprise. As the saying goes they were caught with their pants down. The pants were as far down as their ankles. They were also flat-footed; clueless and impotent to manage blizzards— in Denver of all places.

On another day at the same notorious airport, I had to make my connecting flight. It was one of those days—winds which the pilot told us may be too strong to land. Only one runway was open to flights because of this typical capricious environment. The plane on its descent was thrown sideways and up and down—like a dog shaking a rabbit it just caught.

We had to abort two approaches and finally, the third time we landed with a loud and sudden thud. The passengers burst into cheers in unison, applauding the skilled pilot for getting us to the ground. I was pleased to be safe, but a thought ran through my head:

Even people who fly in first class experience turbulence.

There are no exemptions —even with many zeros' behind the one in the bank statement of the rich and famous, money cannot save them from turbulence. Nobody is immune.

Winds also may blow a plane off its flight path. In fact, I was told by a pilot friend that often the plane is off its flight path—as often as 97%—due to turbulence and strong winds. But we somehow get to our destination just fine. How could that be?

The answer is simply a constant recalibration. Resilience requires frequent recalibrations along the way. We run into unexpected obstacles and suddenly must make new plans. Like a GPS, we recalibrate. We start again. We come back with a resilient mind and move forward toward a goal using a new angle to get us to our destination. Some landings are aborted, and another approach is tried.

Getting to 100 marathons required quite a few flights; cabs, trains, hotels and some of the most important lessons I learned, I learned at 35, 000 feet.

- **Turbulence on flights may be the same for all the passengers, but each person gets to decide how they want to navigate life's sudden and unexpected turbulences.**

PEOPLE

People are like stained-glass windows.
They sparkle and shine when the sun is out, but when
The darkness sets in, their true beauty is revealed
only when there is light from within.

—Elisabeth Kubler-Ross

The most important thing is to try and inspire
people so they can be great
in whatever they want to do.

—Kobe Bryant

HELLO SIS!!

It was a very early and sunny Monday morning when I found myself on a train between Toronto and the Pearson International Airport. The previous day I completed another marathon. I moved slowly and felt a bit stiffer than usual as I settled back into a quiet seat next to my wife who was not amused that we had to get up so early.

It took a while to feel comfortable, but finally I found my sweet spot—almost like a dog that circles a few times before finding the ideal position. Soon I drifted off into a light slumber, rocked by the steady back and forth swaying of the train on its way to Canada's biggest airport.

Suddenly, a cell phone went off *really* loudly and woke me up. The lady who answered the phone seemed very excited and from her immediate answer, "Hello Sis!", I gathered it was her sister on the other end of the line.

The conversation went on for at least half an hour. It felt to me as if the whole train were able to listen in. We gathered that my excited fellow passenger also ran the marathon one day prior to this train ride. It sounded as if it may have been her first ever. She clearly was over-the-moon excited.

A year prior to my train ride a psychiatrist—from Toronto no less—ran a workshop in Kauai. The lecture was on Cognitive Behavioral Therapy. In one of his many entertaining talks Dr. Dubord shared that only 25% of siblings stay in touch regularly with one another when they become adults. I find that rather sad.

In Buddhism there is a term "sympathetic joy." It is one of the four immeasurable minds. (The other three are compassion, kindness and equanimity)

Rather than feel frustrated by my fellow traveler, I was happy for her and her sister. They were sharing a special moment when the odds of being closely connected are only 25%. She obviously did not have to buy in to this truth once spoken by my Life coach: "Friends are God's apology for your family." Clearly her family was the exception.

When I think back to this "Hello Sis!" moment I see how seemingly mundane moments offer us all opportunities to become more skilled at practicing sympathetic joy. The key word is practice.

To cultivate more of the four immeasurable mind-sets takes a lifetime and there is no finish line. We never will reach perfection. But like everyone else I am in the process of growing. I am slowly getting better and better and thus feel good when I pass the test more and more. The day after another marathon in one of my favorite Canadian cities was a personal reminder to:

- **Be glad when others are happy and successful.**

TONY

One of my recent runs took me to an area where I had to cross a railway line. This railway line was busy, but not *that* busy—sort of quiet enough to forget about. It was there that I remembered Tony.

Tony was our handyman. We met him via our neighbor who is a Perfectionist—yes, a capital P perfectionist. The point is that if Tony were good enough for our neighbor whose standards are pretty high, he would *certainly* be good enough for us.

And was he ever good! He was the type of guy who could fix anything. After some runs, I would sit on the deck in our backyard and admire the rock garden he built for us.

Not so long ago on this deck, relaxing after a three-hour run and overlooking Tony's handiwork, I was reading a few pages from a very thoughtful book by Sylvia Boorstein, *Pay Attention for Goodness Sake.* The premise of the book is really the point of this brief story about Tony. It is all about staying aware and awake. To be fully present; not just for your sake, but also the sake of your loved ones.

Building a little landscaped garden next to our deck was one of the last things Tony did for us. He is gone now...transitioned and departed to another realm at a relatively young age. He passed on to another life in his early fifties.

The news of Tony's death still brings tears to our neighbor's eyes and seems surreal to me and my wife when we look upon the great landscaping of our garden. We both say a brief prayer for Tony every time we look upon his work. And when I light a candle before my morning meditations—a ritual I follow because a candle brings light—some days I do that in memory of the light Tony brought to this world by being *truly* helpful.

In addition to working as a handyman and a landscaper, Tony also worked for the railways. One day in the railway yards he had to step outside of his train to do some outside checking. He wore noise protection headphones and it just so happened that on that day he did it without a spotter.

Tony did not hear the train coming toward him. The train ended his life. We miss Tony, but his legacy continues when I sit on my deck or cross railway lines.

- **Always pay close attention even if you never cross railway lines.**

RICHARD DREYFUSS

I was sitting next to a man close to my own age in a bar at a boutique hotel in downtown San Francisco. The hotel is only a few blocks from Union Square and we have stayed there since the mid-nineties. I will not tell you how affordable it was then compared to the mind-boggling prices today if you want to visit San Francisco. Let's just say San Francisco is becoming less and less affordable to visit.

My companion at the bar looked familiar. I tried not to stare at him too long, worried he may be triggered into a sudden offense. Generally, I don't like to offend strangers. He was looking down at his book. I was looking ever so briefly in his direction through the corner of my eye. He looked *so* familiar. I could not remember where I last saw him.

I was sure I had seen him before. And then, a few minutes later, it dawned on me…. I was sitting next to the actor Richard Dreyfuss.

Little did I know that Richard Dreyfuss and I had a few things in common.

To be honest, it was not Mr. Dreyfuss, but a Dreyfuss look-alike. We started a fascinating conversation while sipping some fine wine from one of the best vineyards of California.

My new acquaintance was the same age as me and I discovered through our stimulating conversation that we had the same goals. Mr. "Dreyfuss" was a lawyer in D.C who was visiting the City by the Bay for the same reason I was—to complete another marathon on his quest to reach 100 marathons. Just like me. Same "insanity"; same goals; same brand of running shoes. It was as if we were brothers from a different mother.

It was a bit of a miracle that two humans with so much in common by "accident" were seated next to each other at this bar. I am not aware of too many men our age whose goal it is to finish 100 marathons and then continue with more to come.

We stayed in touch for a few years after our "chance encounter." I believe I reached the mark of 100 marathons before my Dreyfuss buddy, but he did all his 100 races *much faster* than me. What is the point though of comparing and competing when in fact we all are in the same space, doing different things, but with similar goals in the end?

In that bar, with the almost incessant sirens of firetrucks and ambulances racing past our hotel, I learned that:

- **You don't have to subscribe to the notion of synchronicity, but when you see enough "co-incidences", consider if it may be true. In this universe there are no "accidents."**

MY TEACHER, THE CAB DRIVER

Many of the best lessons I have learned over a lifetime were taught by cab drivers. When I sit in the back of a taxicab or Uber, I am all ears… always expecting to get *one* more insight from the driver.

I have found that almost every driver can tell if one is genuinely interested in them. As Dale Carnegie reminded his students…it is skillful to always talk in terms of another person's interest. Human nature, Carnegie said, is basically selfish. Most of us, when looking at a group photo, first look at ourselves—to see if our smile is fine, if our eyes are open or closed, and if our hair is in place.

So I have learned that when one talks in terms of the cab driver's interest, one learns lots.

Not so long ago from the driver's seat of a cab, en route to O'Hare Airport in Chicago, a man originally from Korea, gave me a 30 minute "lecture" on why it is wise to eat lots of fat and zero carbs. He explained that he had diabetes and high blood pressure.

Doctors prescribed all kinds of medications and many had side-effects. None of these doctors were able to help him or meet his expectations. I did not tell him that I was a medical doctor!

His story was amazing because he had wonderful outcomes because of his dietary habits. At least over the short-term. As a medical expert and a doctor who took extra time after medical school to learn more about nutrition, I can go deep here about the pros and cons of various diets, but the story is not about science…it is about learning from cab drivers.

One of my mentors is Dr. Jerry Jampolsky, the founder of Attitudinal Healing. He compiled a list of Twelve Principles of Attitudinal Healing. One of the principles states, "We are students and teachers to one another."

It is useful to read these words, but to experience it in the presence of cab drivers more than once on my way to marathons, conferences, or airports exceeds the mere reading of these words. And even if the driver's advice were sincere and no doubt true for him, I had to base my own wisdom on what is known as experiential wisdom. We may not always agree with our teachers, but at least when we listen deeply, we learn how others think.

Even when I am not in the back of a taxicab, I remember this:

- **Never miss an opportunity to learn from another traveler on this adventure called "life."**

TWO TEACHERS

In 2015 I decided to stop dreaming and act.

I used to be a Dale Carnegie instructor in the 1990's and due to a very busy clinic, and raising a young family, I had to put that on hold around the turn of the century. We all know what it is like to put things on hold and hoping to return to it later…often, we fail to return.

And so it was with teaching the Dale Carnegie training—something that energized me deeply. I never returned to teach this very useful course. I do wear an instructors ring though. It reminds me to live the principles Carnegie taught. They are timeless. They work if you work them.

But ever since the turn of the century, I also wanted to learn more about what it would be like to be a part-time life coach, and in 2015 I met a well-known life coach instructor, Alan Cohen, face-to-face in Hawaii.

Alan is one of the wisest and most soothing sages on the planet. His voice is uniformly admired as peaceful, uplifting, and inspiring. He was born to meet people where they are at. He is extremely gifted in lifting them up, regardless of where they may be during their struggles to find purpose and meaning in their lives.

While doing my training in Hawaii, I kept up the morning ritual of running every day at dawn.

The mind is a curious instrument. I shall never forget the moment Alan taught the class that we only have two simple options: to listen to the voice of fear or to pay closer attention to the voice of love. It must have seeped deep into the inner recesses of my mind, because one morning, during a run, my mind recalibrated itself automatically when I was tempted to harbor negative thoughts about myself. Instantly I became aware of the voice of fear.

We all have been there when we say things about ourselves we would not dare to say about our best friend. The voice of fear tried to convince me that I was a fraud; that people did not really know the real me. On and on it went as I covered one mile after another.

> Then suddenly I rounded a corner and saw a most intense double rainbow hovering over a cemetery.

Suddenly that morning in Hawaii I rounded a corner and saw a most intense double rainbow hovering over a cemetery.

I switched channels immediately and tuned in to the voice of Love. I wondered who created this rainbow; I wondered who determines when we live and when we die; I wondered why I was so blessed to be a student of Alan's. I sensed that what my teacher called Love, is the One that *truly* knows me; an invariable Force and Higher Power who never changes.

All of us were born to be truly helpful. Our factory settings are to be compassionate to one another, but we all have moments where sometimes we lose our way. We forget to be good.

Socrates said it so well when he said the perfect human being is all human beings put together. I often wondered about those words at the start of bigger marathons when I was merely one human among 40,000 others.

Probably not by accident, on the same day as my mind was lost in thoughts of why we are here, I ran past an old church in a village close to the location where we got trained by Alan.

I took a photo of what I saw: a statue of Jesus with his arms wide open, inviting us to come to Him to be taught how to really love one another. All of us matter. There are simply no exceptions. Jesus may not have said it, but I believe He meant to remind us that every encounter with another human should be seen as sacred.

I also remembered that Alan shared a line from *A Course in Miracles* which paraphrased says, "All of God's children are special, but none of God's children are more special."

Some days we may be a student and another day we are a teacher. When we look at people who irritate us, we can reframe them as our teacher also. They may be placed in our path to help us develop patience or forgiveness or compassion. As Alan also taught me a minus is half of a plus. So take the voice of fear, a minus, and turn it into a monumental plus by drawing a vertical line!

That morning in Hawaii I learned that:

- **Life can be simplified when we remember we have only two teachers—love or fear. My favorite teacher is the Voice of Love.**

IS EVERYTHING OK?

I was standing at a desk in the lobby of my hotel in downtown San Francisco, when I heard a distant and rather dejected voice asking this question: "Is everything OK?"

I turned back and noticed a ragged-looking, dirty, and dishevelled human being standing at the front door of the small boutique hotel, holding a Styrofoam cup in his weathered and wrinkled shaking hand. For a moment, a whiff of stale urine emanated from his tired body. He just stood there for a while—radiating a sense of desperateness. Hopelessness probably filled his sad heart. Ignored by the clerk who oversaw the hotel at that moment he asked once more, and this time with much more intensity… "Is everything OK?"

Suddenly, in a pivotal moment, the clerk did not ignore him any longer. Abruptly she commanded him to leave. She chased him away and shut the door in his face. His last feeble words, before the door slammed shut were, "All I wanted was a cup of coffee please."

I was in the city to run my 111th marathon. When I run every day, I usually observe my environment with a keen sense of awareness—regardless of where I run.

To run in San Francisco is to run past hundreds of homeless people. It has gotten worse over the years. I read recently that some residents are suing the city because they are fed up with the way street people there have disrupted what was once pristine and normal.

It was in the same city in a very crowded tourist area where it dawned on me for the first time: with all these various cultures and colored skins present …what if I could look at all humans as if they were either a brother or a sister?

> I remembered Mother Teresa suggesting that all suffering people are Jesus disguised as another human being.

I remembered Mother Teresa suggesting that all suffering people are Jesus disguised as another human being. The same Jesus she mentioned is the one who said, "As much as you have done it to least of these you have done it to me." I hear it said that looking into every face of another human being experiencing deep, deep suffering could be me or you looking directly in the eyes of Jesus himself. I am haunted by those words. Even to this day and probably for many days to come this idea will haunt me. Mother Teresa was so right about that image.

In Zen there is a teaching of lovingkindness meditation. One of the goals of this meditation is simply to be more friendly—toward oneself, loved ones, friends, acquaintances, people who are hard to get along with, and finally every living being on the planet.

"So what could I do about it all?" I wondered to myself as my running route took me through the canyons of the skyscrapers of downtown San Francisco's financial district where hundreds of homeless people, tormented by their own inner demons, lay scattered in a drunken stupor on frigid sidewalks.

The day before the marathon in San Francisco I sensed a deep feeling of community with thousands of other marathoners preparing to run the race the next day. I wished them all this wish: *May you be happy and free from suffering. May you be safe. May you be healthy. May you live at ease.*

As for the homeless man? It was too late to offer him a cup of coffee. He was long gone. I did however send him the same metta meditation of lovingkindness, wishing him to be happy. To this day I remember him and apply lovingkindness meditation, hoping that somehow he will be able to find a way out of his miserable suffering.

Metaphysically I believe there is no 3D reality in true spirituality. So often when I replay that scene in the lobby of my San Francisco hotel…I send this man virtual hugs; metaphysical hugs.

He once was a baby who had a caregiver who changed his diaper. Tonight, he may sleep alone and fitfully on a dark sidewalk along the foggy, breezy, and cold streets of downtown San Francisco.

As I think back to my missed opportunity to be kind to others, I was reminded of the words in the Talmud: "The highest form of wisdom is kindness." And as Mark Twain observed, "Kindness is the language that the blind can see and deaf can hear."

After my encounter in the hotel lobby with the homeless man, I did something people say tourists in San Francisco should never do: I handed the next beggar a $20 bill because at that moment when our eyes met, I heard these words in my mind… "*There but for the Grace of God go I.*"

The suffering homeless man in the lobby taught me:

- **When all is obviously not ok, do your best to alleviate suffering.**

LOOKING INTO THE MIRROR

I belong to a group of ten men. They have taught me several lessons. The main lesson, by far, is that we all grow together when we take turns to investigate the mirror.

I first met them indirectly via my doctor who sees me only for routine check-ups. So far, I have had the good fortune of completing over 100 marathons without encountering serious health issues or a need to see a doctor for urgent matters.

My doctor told me he belongs to a men's group which pursues excellence in all areas—spirit, mind, and body. One day after visiting the good doctor, I received an invitation to join this fine group of men —all of them mentors to me in so many ways. All of these men pursue the cultivation of deeper spiritually.

We do not use real mirrors of course, because we are tough men who tend to focus on results more than our actual physical looks.

> By holding up a mirror, we take turns to look at our individual lives...examining if we are moving forward or not.

By holding up a figurative mirror, we take turns to reflect more clearly about our individual lives...examining if we are moving forward or not. We look at our lives in terms of family, health, work, personal progress, and above all...our spiritual habits.

What we see is not always ideal. None of the men blame the mirror. The mirror merely reflects our truths and energies. Sometimes it looks great and at other times not so good.

Neither do the men judge each other—we have a great sense of unity, respect, and trust.

We keep one another accountable and encourage each other to have the right thoughts about *all* aspects of our lives. To me these guys always look great because as Roald Dahl observed, "If you have good thoughts, they will shine out on your face, like sunbeams, and you will always look lovely."

The Dalai Lama once said it is wise to spend some time alone at least once every day. Call it quiet time; mirror time; alone time; morning rituals; or whatever you choose to call it…but for your sake and the sake of those you serve please do it. Just do it. Do it regularly.

- **Stay accountable but make sure of two things: always make sure the mirror does not distort reality and be sure that those you choose to be open with are trustworthy**

THE CONFUSING TEXT MESSAGE

I am sure it has happened to you too—at least once—where someone sends you a text. They may not be in your contacts, and thus it is only a number that shows up, with no name linked to it.

You wonder who this is. Do you text back or do you let it go?

My phone lit up early one morning just before I left our home to head out into Arctic air for a run. The text was brief and confusing: *Hey Dr. Nieman, I was wondering if I can come over to your place and do a film clip on you for my project.*

What was this about? Was there an urgency? When did this person want to come over? What exactly was "my project?"

Naturally, I had to text back: *I am so sorry. I have no idea what this text is about. Can you please give me a bit more information?*

The person on the other end must have been glued to his phone because seconds later I was up to speed when he texted back. It was Jacob.

Jacob has been one of my patients since shortly after his birth. When I think of my older patients, I am reminded how quickly time can fly. I remember Jacob as a kind and intelligent human being, and as a super-dedicated sports enthusiast even from a very young age. His mom told me that her son was dreaming of being a famous anchor on a sports channel one day.

I discovered that Jacob was now in college and studying media. One of his assignments was to find an interesting athlete and pretend he was running a two-minute story for the evening news. Jacob informed me that as soon as his professor mentioned "interesting athlete" my name immediately came to mind.

I was surprised. I have never thought of myself in that context. I just see myself as a very fortunate fellow who can do what he enjoys so much, experiencing motion as a tool to create fresh energy every day of his life.

It was the dead of winter when Jacob knocked on my door one late afternoon around five. Because the days are so short in winter, the sun was already close to setting. There was a crispness to the air when I opened the door and stepped outside. When I exhaled, my breath created a lingering mist.

For the next hour or so Jacob interviewed me and took shots of me running back and forth. I found myself obeying this young teen as he "directed" me outside on pathways cleared by the city from slick ice and snow. The white snowbanks along the pathway looked bigger than they were when Jacob leaned down low with his nifty camera. He was trying to take some unusual angles for additional visual effects.

The warm air expelled by my exhales created a cloud of steam coming out of my mouth. I was glad I wore some gloves because my hands were getting a bit blue in the cold. If I were alone, I would have worn ski goggles to keep my eyeballs warm. Googles are my way of overcoming windchill factors as cold as 20 below or worse.

Fortunately, Jacob got his key shots done in no time and we went indoors for more questions and for him to take what is called "B Rolls" in media— shots not of the person, but of things such as medals from various marathons and photos of past races decorating the walls of my warm and cozy study.

My Boston marathon finish photo was taken when I was still ignorant of how important it is to look up rather than look down upon crossing the finish line. That seminal moment for me could have been better had I looked up, but at the end of my first ever Boston marathon I was too tired to remember such minute detail! Jacob hovered his camera over this photo in my study a bit longer than the other photos.

Later I received a USB stick with the amazing clip this talented young man did of his doctor, running all over the place and having fun. It warmed my heart. Suddenly that text message became a special one out of dozens that day. Thoughts about Jacob made me feel old and reminded me how quickly time flies by.

Now when I feel the occasional early-warning signs of old age some days, I tend remember that clip, Jacob's clip, and it always helps me to reflect on this key truth:

- **Although it is 100% certain we will all age and none of us will escape death…the truth is that we have some influence in slowing down our aging process.**

DAVE

About 20 years ago—long before I decided to become a streaker, never missing a day of running—I was on TV almost every other week as a medical contributor to the local morning TV show in a city of 1.2 million people.

I always enjoyed going into the studio to be with Dave, the popular host of The Breakfast Show. Dave is one of those humans who attracts all kinds of people because of his charismatic personality. The default setting on Dave's face is a perpetual grin. I have never seen him frown or get angry. He is one of the few people I have met who is consistently flawless when it comes to thinking on one's feet and improvising when the unexpected happens.

I have observed that some people live their lives like pop with no fizz. "Flat Coke" some call it. Others, like Dave, are constantly full of bubbles.

They sparkle day in and day out. Enthusiasm is their middle name. No matter the type of weather of the day, every day for them is an up day. They look upon every day as an opportunity to show up fully and brighten the lives of many others—on purpose, yet effortlessly. They bring out the best in all and make people feel noticed and appreciated.

One dreary, rainy morning I entered the TV studio. It was still dark outside. Inside the studio there was a warm energy and just before we went on the air, Dave leaned over and asked me about my running. He knew I was a runner, and he was proud to inform me that he too had taken up running not that long ago. Dave's face was beaming. Clearly, he found a new way to recreate and improve his energy.

The camera man counted down with his hand in the air so we could see the countdown from five fingers to four to three to two to one and then we were on the air.

The topic of the interview that day escapes me now, but I shall never forget what happened when we were done.

Dave agreed to run a marathon with me! At first, he was looking for all kinds of excuses to cop out, but I could tell his eyes were curious. It was as if they signalled these words in my direction: *I wonder what would happen if I trained for a marathon? I wonder if I can do it? I wonder what it would be like to get a medal around my neck at the finish line and what will I do with the medal? Should I make this run not about me, but about raising money for charity?*

A few months later Dave and I lined up at the start of the Calgary Marathon.

I am not sure it helps to have the name Dave when you want to be funny, but Dave had something in common with David Letterman: he could literally see something funny in anything, including traffic lights. It is an amazing skill I admire in comedians: the ability to look at the mundane and make a joke out of it. We see lights and they look at the same lights and see humor.

It just so happened that most of the traffic lights at the intersections were green when we passed those spots. One intersection after another. Of course, if they were red it would not matter. Roads are closed on marathon day and police are there to ensure the safety of runners and spectators. As runners we are also grateful for the way the police deal with the ever-predictable impatient drivers who do not give a rip about runners and the money raised by those running for a charity. Instead, these drivers just care about themselves.

Dave leaned over to me and said with a wide grin on his face, "Doc, it's a good thing we are hitting all the green lights today!"

Along the way many spectators recognized him, the local celebrity, and shouted "Way to go Dave." Dave was famous and I was not, so the sociologist in me was intrigued to hear all the comments coming from spectators who lined the course...until we got to 23 miles.

Around that mark Dave asked if it was OK to "drop me." He felt strong and wanted to come in just under four hours. He did it, and I was not too far behind. I could not have been happier for him when I met him at the finish line.

Dave insisted that we had to get our photo taken together after the run. And typical for a guy in media he told me to remove my dark glasses so that our happy eyes were not obscured! Only Dave would have thought about that, being aware of how to improve a photo or a clip on TV.

Ever since then when I am in my car and get red lights instead of green traffic lights, it reminds me to pause and be grateful for whatever positive things come to mind. I often see it like this:

- **If you get a lot of green lights be thankful. If you get a lot of red lights be thankful too. They offer you a pause to practice intentional gratitude.**

THE EXAMPLE

When I head out of the door—95% of the time in the mornings—for my daily runs, I have noticed how what happened the day before seems to be a theme which dominates my thinking. Often it has to do with another person who left a deep impression on me the previous day.

Recently a youth Pastor, Randy Cater, showed up to watch my 16-year-old son, Benjamin, play an important rugby game. Randy has an ever-overflowing full plate, and yet he made the time to cheer Ben on from the sidelines—almost like a second father. As a devout follower of the teachings of Christ, and always looking for ways to be supportive, Randy's sincere kindness called to mind a poem by Edgar Guest, named "Sermons We See."

This poem is kept on my phone to share with others whenever the time is right:

I'd rather see a sermon than hear one any day;
I'd rather one should walk with me than merely tell the way.
The eye is a better pupil and more willing than the ear,
Fine counsel is confusing, but example is always clear;
And the best of all the preachers are the men who live their creeds,
For to see good put in action is what everybody needs.

The poem goes on and adds, "One deed of kindness noticed is worth forty that are told."

In the Buddhist tradition there is a meditation known as "Metta". It involves lovingkindness expressed to oneself and others. It matches and aligns with the teachings of Jesus who taught that we must pray for our enemies, but also, that we are not selfish if we pray for ourselves.

Randy is a youth pastor but never preaches to people he meets in public. His example reminds me that Saint Augustine said that we must always preach with our lives, and only if absolutely necessary, use words.

Randy's example to me and the practice of metta meditation both inspired me and served as lessons: there is a time to run for the sake of running, being fully present in the moment, moving forward at a pace and direction that suits my level of fitness…but there also are times to reflect, while running, on the daily choices that lie ahead after the run is done. Often, I frame it as a question: *What is truly needed here?*

Randy also taught me to not ask others "How are you?" but rather ask them "How is your heart today?"

As one of my many mentors, the late Dr. Wayne Dyer, used to teach: "When deciding to be right or kind…choose kind."

- **Know when and how to be fully present. Set this as an intention before you choose how to live the day that stretches ahead of you**

COMMUNITY

I once heard one of my spiritual coaches, Dr. Len Zoeteman, teach on the topic of community.

He said that the word community can be also summed up as saying "Common Unity."

I trust that the next few stories will make you see how that is true.

Dr. Peter Nieman

CONNECTION

I have had the distinct honor over almost four decades of being a doctor, to help families stay healthy. When I am with my patients there always seems to be a common connection. I become deeply aware of our common humanity.

I never took that honor lightly because the love of a parent for a child is boundless. For any parent to trust me with this task of caring and being helpful is something I have never taken for granted. So many parents brought their fears to me over the years. It had to do with their own flesh and blood, their dear children, far, far more than themselves.

My job can be described as a pattern-spotter. If one spots the same patterns over and over and in independent scenarios… and one notices one common over-lap, then it is probably the truth.

Not only is it a truth, but it is a universal and timeless truth.

Here is the truth: most humans like to belong. In Maslow's hierarchy of human needs, belonging ranks quite high. Loneliness in our era has become the new norm for many. I am aware of research which tells us that being lonely is as bad a smoking a pack of cigarettes daily.

It is sad to think how many lonely children have many internet friends but at the same time lose hope and get overwhelmed by the facts that nobody wants to be a true friend. Self-harm becomes an escape hatch for far too many young people who suffer because they do not yet feel they belong. They give up trying to make connections. They quit by ending their lives.

Many people have friends and yet *even* in crowds they still feel lonely.

Whenever I am asked what I make of huge crowds at marathons, my mind immediately transports me back to one cool, but sunny morning on Staten Island in New York, where I certainly did not feel alone at all.

Close to 40,000 runners lined up in the starting area of the New York City Marathon. I looked at the shiny Atlantic Ocean toward the east and then turned to the west, only to be almost blinded by the golden glare of the bright morning sun bouncing off the windows of the tall skyscrapers that make New York City, New York City.

I close my eyes and I can still hear Frank Sinatra's song *New York, New York* and the words, *"If you can make it there, you can make it anywhere."*

In front of me and behind me stretched a sea of colorful marathon runners. Once again, I was struck by these words: common humanity. We all were bonded by one goal: to have fun and finish the race. We took the time to enter. It was the same choice for all those present. We all had feelings, dreams, and hopes. We were all human and regardless of race, creed, or gender the distance was going to be the same for all—26.2 miles.

Many times, when I run in various parts of the world and pass another runner, we say hello. We wave and we smile (except during tough marathons where some of us look down and simply want to be left alone as we wallow in our suffering and wonder why we do this to begin with).

There is indeed a running community. We share a common unity.

> Find out where you belong and be there as often as possible.

In Canada, a community started in a very small room, many decades ago in Edmonton. This space was about half the size of a tennis court. The store, now known in North America as "The Running Room" still exists. The brand has mushroomed all over the place in two countries.

It grew because it created communities of runners linked by a common goal—to run.

In our neighborhood I know a good man called Sean who is also a runner. In 2017 he was part of a group of 112 people who ran in a local marathon, but this run was unusual and on purpose. Sean was part of a community of runners who were tied together by a rope. The goal was to break the Guinness World Record of running a marathon tied together to raise money for research on mitochondrial diseases. Mitochondria are the cells in our body known as energy factories.

The youngest runner in the group was 15 and the oldest was 80. They became one. They energized all the other runners who were part of the race. How they took bathroom breaks is another story for another time.

Since then, their record was broken and at the time of this writing the record for the number of runners tied together while completing a marathon stands at 122. Sean's record may be broken, but what is not broken are the sweet memories he still shares of what it meant to be part of that community on that day—he still stays in touch with some of the runners in that group. They remain connected. They share a common unity to this day.

Like various Catholics around the globe gathering together to celebrate mass, runners from all over the world gather together in marathons on a quest to test their endurance. On a specific day, the motive is the same for all. There is a common unity. There is bonding where all are equal regardless of backgrounds. The distance is the same for all—26.2 miles.

How often can you say you truly feel fully connected? Connected to your own thoughts and awareness, connected to the needs of others, and connected to the environment? Some would simply refer to this state as having a common unity.

I am no theologian; I am not a professor of philosophy at Harvard; I am not a mystic; I am not a guru.

I am a runner and a fellow traveller...and this is what running taught me: There will be moments when you will look at the crowds in New York or Chicago (40,000 plus) and you will see a sea of people. And just as the branches of the same tree are different, yet connected, so the people are different, yet connected. Kinship with other humans is also like looking at my hand and seeing five fingers all belonging to the same hand.

- **Find out where you belong; be there as often as possible...and it may just save a few lives.**

NEVER ALONE

I almost called this book "Almost There!" Please note the exclamation mark. I have heard that phrase loud and clear hundreds of times from numerous spectators lining the 26.2 miles of a marathon *anywhere* in the world.

A marathon is 26.2 miles which is 42.2 kilometers. Only people who never ran a marathon will tell runners at the five mile mark, "Looking strong… you are almost there!"

I understand that spectators can be well-meaning, but really…say that when I am bleeding all over the place, sweating like a fountain, with jelly legs, light-headed and resisting the urge to puke, or battling with the temptation to quit at mile 25!

One of greatest experiences in running marathons is to interact with a supporting crowd.

In New York City, there are only a few places where crowds are not allowed along the marathon route. One such place is the bridge which takes runners from Queens into Manhattan. But this quiet zone does not last long. No sooner does one set foot on Manhattan and the crowds roar deeply and wave colorful balloons as if their lives depend on it. Kids stretch forth their hands to receive a reciprocal touch from various runners—total strangers. And yet experiencing some form of bonding.

During the Boston Marathon, around the half way mark, one can hear the distant noise *way* before one passes Wellesley College. Here the female students are kept behind barricades to "protect" runners. I have done Boston twice and both times I momentarily experienced what the Beatles and other celebrities must have felt…excited crowds almost too close for comfort.

The Houston Marathon is one of the best marathons for humor. Spectators hold up signs all along the 26.2 miles that distract runners from their "suffering". One sign I shall always remember—perhaps because my work involves helping people not be constipated due to improper eating habits—is a sign which read: "Run like you are having a bowel movement; take it easy at the start and press hard toward the end."

Although spectators come out from the side-lines to encourage runners, in the end they cannot run the race for the athletes. But combine the grit and determination of an athlete with the crowd support and the odds of finishing strong become that much higher.

Who do you have in your corner? Who is sitting in the front row applauding you and leading the standing ovation? If you struggle to identify those people in your life, do not give up. Move forward, trusting that when the student is ready the teacher will indeed arrive.

Sometimes you may feel that you will never get there but allow me to remind you that you too are almost there. By saying almost there I mean that almost is not going to happen soon, but when you hang in there; when you endure; when you stay patient; when you take things one step at time…when you do all this you too are almost there. It is just a matter of time. Hang in there. Stay strong. Refuse to listen to the negative Nellies.

Refuse to listen to the voice of fear. Choose to switch to another channel: the reception there is way clearer. The picture is in high definition and crystal clear.

When I was a kid in Africa, I tuned in to what was then called short wave radio. We had to adjust the radio's antenna to better receive what was called *The Voice of America*.

But today I encourage you to change to another channel. I call that channel *The Voice of HOPE.*

- **It may seem that we reach goals on our own, but the reality is that we are interconnected with others. You are never alone. You are sustained. Keep moving forward.**

UNITY

Tough times caused by pandemics, power failures, hurricanes, and wildfires have one thing in common: they all cause a common-unity. Community.

When we are intimate with others, sharing our pains and victories, we arrive at a place of intimacy—some have coined it "into--me –see".

I have run all over the planet, but one thing that really impressed me was the common themes we all share—regardless of where we live.

People who live in Hawaii are familiar with the Aloha Oath* which talks about being fellow members of a greater community. During one of my visits to Hawaii I read this Oath:

I solemnly promise to live every heartbeat of my life

From this day forward with pure Aloha

Every single word that comes from my mouth

> *And every single action, be it large or small*
> *Must first come from my compassionate heart*
> *And be supported by my thoughtful mind*
> *With an open heart and an open mind*

---

* (For a complete version of the oath see www.houseofpurealhoa.com/the-pure-aloha-oath)

We all belong to a *human* race and every one of us runs their own metaphysical race uniquely.

The detail of our daily choices may vary. Branches of the same tree vary from branch to branch—yet they are connected to the *exact* same tree.

One of the key teachings of the Buddhist tradition is called interconnectedness. Some Buddhist writers also refer to this as "Interbeing". Metaphors are used by teachers to make their point: can one wave in the vast ocean claim it is separate from all the other waves of the ocean?

In my 65 cycles around the sun, my deepest sense of connectedness came from being with thousands of other runners. These are moments where I observed the diversity of others and yet we were the same. We all bleed the same color blood when we are cut, regardless of being male or female; black or white; tall or short; handsome and less handsome; fat or thin.

> Can one wave in the vast ocean claim it is separate from all other waves of the ocean?

And so, at the start and finish of so many marathons, I found myself in waves upon waves of humanity at the starting line of a 26.2 mile quest to endure in rain, wind, heat, cold, and a few steep inclines mixed into all the above. Together, but at different speeds, we endure just for "fun". Together we learn more about ourselves and the ability to endure to the limit.

One morning at sunrise over Lake Michigan, just before the start of the Chicago Marathon, I learned this key lesson:

- **On the outside we may all be different, but on the inside a brain is a brain and a heart is a heart and we all bleed, bright red blood when we are cut.**

THE MOVING HOUSE

Today I ran by a fabulous home in a highly desirable neighborhood. This neighborhood finds itself in a community where most of the homes are old and yet the location is idyllic and very peaceful.

This older, yet still attractive house, happens to be in a city full of lamentations. The doom and gloom relate to the fact that the economy depends almost entirely on the price of oil and since the oil industry is heading slowly, but surely, closer to the edge of a cliff, the future looks bleak.

Many of the homes in this neighborhood also look totally different from the street than they do from another angle. From the street it looks like a single level home when in fact from the other side there often are two to three levels, all with spectacular views of a lake and mountains in the distance.

Looks indeed may deceive at times and perspective is everything.

> The owners of the house I passed on this particular day, apparently did not pay too much attention to the current narrative of doom and gloom.

The owners of the house I passed on this particular day, apparently did not pay too much attention to the current narrative of doom and gloom.

Or maybe they did not get the memo saying bad times are here to last and may get worse.

They decided to move a perfectly fine home away from the terrific neighborhood so that it could make space for a more contemporary and modern home—with all the bells and whistles that will make even Frank Lloyd Wright drool. The fact that such technology exists to move a two story home intact, impressed me greatly.

Once again running was not just for my muscles, heart, lungs, and brain—it also served as my teacher. I learned that we all get to choose if we want to participate in the narrative of the day...or not.

Along that run I also had a view of tall mountains with snow on the top, almost all year round. Unlike man-made homes, those mountains never move. I was reminded that although we live in a world full of constant change, mountains may be there to teach us that we can find some degree of stability if we are grounded firmly and weather storms with wisdom and compassion.

- **Accept the fact that few things stay the same and that we live in an imperfect world. By refusing to accept this we cause our own suffering.**

LOOKING GOOD!

I have the unfortunate but very true proof via photographs taken along the route of many marathons that I did not look very good at times. Not only did I look tired, but I *felt* that way—never quitting though, because it is just not an option. If I have to leopard crawl my way to the finish line and get there two days later, I would do just that.

I have an Apollo 13 mind. The commander of the spacecraft may have said "failure is not an option" or maybe the ground crew said those words, but either way, over one hundred times, I started a marathon and by the grace of my Creator, I finished them all. Over 100 times I lined up at the starting line and over 100 times, without exception, I crossed the finish line.

> An Australian couple decided that they were going to run 365 marathons in one year—together as a couple. They did it 365 days later.

Just writing this tires me out—the thought that even with God's help I did it. Yet it is perhaps not as impressive as the story of a husband and wife, both endurance runners.

This Australian couple decided on December 31 that they were going to run one marathon a day for one year—together as a couple. They did it 365 days later. They never missed a single day for a whole year. I find this both very amazing and inspiring.

Recently I ran a marathon where a female runner running behind me must have heard the conversation I had with an 80 year-old runner who inspired me. This veteran asked me what number marathon this was for me.

I told him it was a strange number—111. As soon as I said that the runner behind me loudly let out an expletive that cannot be mentioned here.

I smiled and told her about the Ausies who did 365 marathons in one year—together. She did not know what to say. Maybe she was tired, just thinking about the effort involved in such an unusual quest.

Around that time—about ten percent into the race a spectator shouted, "Looking good…you are almost there!"

Runners love encouragement, but at a few miles into the run, we were far, far from almost there.

Enthusiastic crowds can make the time go by faster; one can feel their energy always. But there is one thing they cannot do for us runners—they cannot run our race. If it is going to be, it is up to me.

If it is going to be it is up to me, is an expression which at first may sound very egotistical, but it is not. Those words remind me of my personal responsibility in life—free will as some would choose to name it.

From personal experience, I am completely convinced that we and we *alone* decide how we will run. Nobody runs on our behalf. Even when we are surrounded by crowds, we are lonely in some sense and not looking good at times—both inside and outside.

It helps to stick with buddies. The running community taught me this when I was around ten years old. I lived where the Comrades Marathon takes place every year—it is one of the world's most famous long-distance runs. The name was chosen to make the point that we endure better when we do it together. As many wise poets and authors all observed—and I paraphrase here— a rope made of three cords is not easily broken.

And the looking good part? As I said, photos tell a different story. It is hard work—especially at 26 miles when there are 0.2 miles left. (I was told that marathons used to be 26 miles but at one Olympic Games the race ended close to Buckingham Palace The King wanted to see the finish, so organizers added another 0.2 miles for the King's sake.)

These well-meaning spectators who tried to uplift the runners taught me a valuable lesson I use in my clinic with patients who have lost hope and who are tired.

- **When we encourage others and do it to help them, make sure that the encouragement is based on reality and not false hope.**

BODY

Take care of your body.
It is the only place you have to live

—Jim Rohn

REST

One of my friends who feels free to call me when he needs help coping with the ups and downs of life is a sleep specialist. We have shared many deep conversations during easy runs. Not only does our running connect us; our tears have also connected us.

When I listen to his wisdom on how sleep matters the most—perhaps *the* most in determining our energy and wellness— I am amazed that modern medicine did not have a formal sleep training path until relatively recently.

The so-called father of sleep medicine, one of my friend's great role models and mentors, passed away at the time of writing this book. In the obituary of Dr. William Dement we are told that when he worked as a medical researcher in the 1950's, the topic of sleep caused many to yawn, scientifically speaking. It was boring then. Dement founded the American Academy of Sleep Medicine and was instrumental in teaching the world about the critical role of restful sleep.

Of course, as a doctor I can go off on a tangent here about the cycles and stages of sleep, the science of sleep and much more. But this book is not about the "boring" detail; it is meant to get you to enjoy simple stories and simple lessons born out of ideas generated by exercise. It is singularly focused on discovering ways to guide us in our quest to move forward to our unique finish lines, one step at a time. Ironically, it is our skillful resting that gets us there.

So, allow me to share an entertaining story about Dr. Dement. Apparently, he was passionate about his teaching and sharing information with new doctors. I have noticed that many successful movements, revolutions, or organizations prioritized the teaching of the next generation. What the wiser and experienced sages already discovered was skillfully shared with the youth in their communities.

Dement, I discovered, would grant extra credits to students who nodded off in his undergraduate sleep class. He would wake them up with a squirt gun and urge them to stand and declare, "Drowsiness is red alert!"

To be woken up to the truth that although we may be getting A's for healthy nutrition habits, and high marks for exercise and attitude, but strike out when it comes to proper and timely rest…to clearly see the value of regular rest, let us *never* forget a line by Dale Carnegie who wrote:

- **It is wise to rest before we get tired.**

FITBUTT

There is a well-known fitness tracker tool made by Fitbit, a company based out of San Francisco. I am a loyal fan of this tool. But I am also a fan of the Fitbutt principle.

Many people get off their butts and yet…they die at an early age because they thought that being fit means you are insured against an early exit; they never expected that they would end up fertilizing daffodils before their exit was supposed to happen.

About two years into my running career, which at the time of this writing stretches over thirty years, I discovered this truth for the first time: you can be physically fit but *still* be unhealthy. Fitness does not automatically mean health.

I read about Jim Fixx who illustrates this concept very well. Jim was known in the running world as *the* person who originally put running on the map. When visiting the Cooper Clinic in Dallas, he was invited to be studied while running on a treadmill. The idea was to see how long he could last. Jim refused to do this and walked away with these words coming out of his mouth: "I know I am fit and there is no need to test me and tell me what I already know."

A short while later a heart attack ended Fixx's life in a matter of seconds. The running community was shocked and at a loss for words—dumped into total disbelief and wondering *if it could happen to a man like Fixx, can it happen to anyone? Was exercise not supposed to reduce some of the risks?*

My own running coach recently called me from a hospital bed. He was a bit luckier than Fixx. His warning signs were unusual fatigue and once his wife took him to the ER, he was diagnosed with severe coronary artery disease. This problem required surgery as the only way to resolve it.

One can think of obese people who do not run much if at all. They have a paunch and high blood pressure and yet their destiny is to live longer than athletes. So what is up? Where is the truth or at least the latest science?

I am not sure one can explain this completely and logically. Of course cardiologists think they know--and I am sure they know a lot-- but I read that even when he was regularly assessed as the President of the USA, Bill Clinton's *severely* blocked coronary vessels went undiagnosed.

The story I am about to share, makes me wonder if we should simply do our best and hope our destiny is like the man in the following newspaper story.

The newspaper headline read, *"Surgeon who saved hiker later operates on his heart"*. This caught my attention, because it took place in an area I often hike in when I find myself in the mountains one hour west of where we live.

The story went on to say, "Calgarian Darrell Parker has taken the idea of having a personal physician to heart. In a nine-day span, Parker was resuscitated by Dr. Corey Adams, only to have the cardiac surgeon perform a quintuple bypass procedure to finish the job."

The surgeon was hiking in the same area as Mr. Parker that day and noticed a commotion of a man being given CPR. When the surgeon noticed that the victim had no pulse and was completely blue, he put his experience to work. Parker survived and was transferred to a major hospital in Calgary.

Nine days later the same surgeon, who administered CPR in the remote part of the mountains, performed a 4.5 hour operation on the same hiker he once found pulseless and blue.

Parker later observed "It's divine intervention…there is some Higher Power working on me. We are more than happy it worked out the way it did."

My life coach taught me that there are many people who may like the ideas one offers them as a coach…and yet they may have a habit of responding: "Yes but!". They never seem to run out of excuses. They are full of lies when they rationalize. A motivational speaker once told his audience "Rationalize should be spelled rational-lies".

When it comes to preventing heart disease exercise is not enough. We also must focus on eating healthier and controlling stress. We know that. We even verbally admit it and add our "Ya-but" afterwards.

Alan Cohen teaches his life coach students to allow their clients only three "Yes buts", and then tell the client, "You have used up all your buts, now get off your butt and get busy."

Even though I am a doctor who runs marathons and tries hard to stay out of trouble, I am often reminded that there is such a thing as destiny, but we also play a role in the trajectory of our destinies by remembering that:

- **You can be fit…but also unhealthy.**

AGING

In 1994 an interesting person crossed my path in Dallas at the world-famous Cooper Clinic. I was in Dallas to run my first ever Dallas Marathon.

I met Johnny Kelley in person and was amazed by such an opportunity. Prior to my Dallas marathon, I only knew about him via a book titled *Young at Heart*. Writing the foreword for this book the father of aerobics, Dr. Ken Cooper wrote, "Johnny is a truly unique torchbearer for marathoning and aerobics in general."

Johnny became famous because of the Boston marathon and his extreme fitness when he was deep into his senior years. In 1991 at the "tender" age of 83, Johnny ran the Boston marathon in five hours and 42 minutes. Few athletes have the terrier-like tenacity it takes to endure and sustain fitness for as long as Johnny did.

He is known as Boston's Marathon Man. The famous author and runner George Sheehan said of Kelley, "Runners and anyone else in the race of life, seeking a mentor to guide them on their own epic quest, need look no further."

When I met Kelley he told me his visit to the Cooper clinic had a purpose: experts in sport medicine were to measure the fitness capacity of someone in his eighties. Kelley obviously subscribed to the notion of "what we treasure we must measure."

It is indeed true that all of us have been given various genes to work with, but our lifestyles dance with these genes and the outcome varies tremendously depending on the lifestyle we choose to cultivate.

In one of Dale Carnegie's famous books, *How to Stop Worrying and Start Living*, he tells a story of a destitute woman who once knocked on the door of a stranger on a cold October night shortly after the Civil War. The owner, a widow, felt sorry for this stranger and allowed the uninspiring and frail soul into her home.

When a relative of the owner came up from New York to the New England region for a visit, he discovered this strange guest and demanded that she leave. He shoved the homeless woman out of the door and into the cold driving rain where she stood shivering for a while before moving on to find shelter somewhere else.

Little did the visitor from New York realize that the "vagabond" would become the founder of Christian Science. The poor "old" lady who was shoved into the cold was Mary Baker Eddy. Mrs. Eddy was instrumental in starting a religious belief system which values the impact of the mind upon our aging process.

As a physician I have always had a deep interest in the power of the mind in terms of athletics and wellness.

There is no doubt that we cannot avoid aging but there are ways to slow down the rate of aging. This is a topic that has been covered by experts and one, Dr Valter Longo from UCLA, stands out from all other experts. Reading his books or watching his You Tube talks provides an abundance of evidence that *we get to choose* how fast or slow we will age.

I read in a United Press International news clip about a California woman who at age 99, became the world's oldest pilot and flight instructor.

Robina Asti, according to the Guinness Book of World Records, was named the world's oldest flight instructor and active pilot when she gave lessons at the Next Gen Flight Academy at the Riverside Municipal Airport in California in 2020. According to UPI, Asti said she wanted to show that senior citizens are still capable of making valuable contributions.

The previous record was held by a 98-year-old man from Iowa.

I believe these elderly examples teach me that there is a big difference between lifespan and healthspan. Most of us have heard about lifespan—the time between birth and passing on to the next life after we die. But what about healthspan?

Healthspan is all about how healthy we are right up to the very end of our lives. As a doctor familiar with lifestyle medicine, it brings me much joy to share ideas on how to harness healthy eating, regular exercise, wise resting, and positive attitudinal living in order to end up with a better chance of a good healthspan.

By the way, for those among us who plan to live a long life, I highly recommend following the same lifestyle as those humans who live in what some call the Blue Zones. In his book with the same title, Dan Buettner explains in minute and scientific detail what the Blue Zones are all about.

I have no desire to pilot planes when I grow up one day, but as a seasoned athlete, still able to run marathons in my sixties, I am hoping that by the grace of God, I can continue to run if I have a beating heart and a willing breath. Meanwhile I have indeed learned that:

- **We get to choose how we want to deal with the inescapable truth of aging.**

GOOD WORK!

The other day I started to use a brand-new fitness tracker. It smelled new as I took it out of the box—almost like a new car or brand-new shoes!

I like it a lot. In fact, I like it so much that at times I take it off *only* when I shower. It helps me monitor my progress in areas I love to track—even when I sleep deeply it works, tracking the duration and quality of my sleep.

But I discovered it also lies—as often as I want it to lie. (At least I get to control its deceptions.)

I discovered that if I activate it to monitor my heart rate, distance, and speed for only three seconds there is always a message as soon as I stop the monitoring which says, "Good Work."

Three seconds in my bed, on my back, and three hours out on a run in sleet, wind, rain, going uphill and both times I get the *same* message… Good work!

> One lap around a standard athletic track is 400 meters. I read a story about a runner who did one lap.

These devices can really control our logic if we let it. One lap around a standard athletic track is 400 meters. I read a story about a runner who did one lap, almost always looking down at his tracker, perhaps missing out on the nice scenery.

When he completed one lap and saw the number on the tracker as 425 meters, he was upset—not because the tracker failed its accuracy test, but because the track was too long in his estimation.

He believed the tracker more than the true reality of a 400 meter track, carefully and accurately measured down to the very last inch.

- **At a time when technology has a more ubiquitous impact on our lives, it is wise to remember to trust it, but only up to a point.**

DENTISTS

I once read somewhere about a man who would rather take some time off work to have root canal surgery done than stay at his office.

If that is the case, I would say it is probably time to look for a new job!

My dad was fond of telling a story about a man who was very worried about seeing a dentist. He equated the dentist with a form of torture and at the very start of the visit, just when the dentist approached him, he grabbed the poor doctor by the gonads and said, "Doc, let us get this straight...we are not going to hurt each other, today are we?"

But some runners need dentists far too often and the reason may surprise you. It certainly surprised me that at the Olympic Games a dental office can be a busy place. Apparently, it has to do with the drinks and sweet gels used during some endurance events.

Marathon runners litter roads—I remember being in DC once on a Sunday afternoon, after the Marine Corps Marathon took place that morning. A good friend of mine who lives in DC wanted to show me the infamous Watergate building. As we walked along the streets around Watergate, I spotted several empty energy gels all over the place. These gels are easy to carry and they are like gold to many runners: forget to pack your gels and you may hit a wall early and hard in the marathon, the victim of a dangerously low glucose level in your bloodstream, already saturated with excessive levels of lactic acid.

To "bonk" is to hit the wall; to hit the wall is to run out of glycogen; to run out of glycogen is…when you forgot to pack your gels. And to forget to pack your gels is to not be fully present. Attentiveness matters a great deal when one aims to tackle a 26.2 mile run.

But other than causing litter, gels cause tooth decay—if used improperly. It is a good idea to add some plain Adam's Ale (water) also.

So, whenever I do exceptionally long runs where an energy gel keeps me from being dizzy, seeing stars and feeling as if I may faint in any moment, I wash my mouth out with lots of water and remember:

- **Some of my best friends are dentists, but I tell them to not take it personally when I say I prefer to see them only for routine check-ups.**

JUST SIT

I feel very guilty when I sit. It got worse since I attended a lecture in Florida many moons ago. The lecture was about red double decker buses in the UK. It is a long story, so bear with me while I try to explain how important it is to sit wisely.

Long before the media became aware of the dangers of sitting, I heard a scientist explain what happened in London, England many decades ago. Researchers looked at the drivers of double decker buses and the conductors. These men were compared in terms of longevity.

It turned out that drivers did not live as long. Conductors who were always on the move—back and forth and up and down the stairs of these iconic red buses—lived quite a bit longer. Why?

Drivers sat and conductors moved.

And so we end up today with headlines screaming at us: "Sitting worse than smoking—the new disease."

I thought I was doing great with my morning runs, but apparently that is not good enough. If one exercises at the start of the day and then sits still for the rest of the day, it does one no good. When we move, our muscles contract and send off hope hormones to our brains, enabling us to be better equipped at handling depression and anxiety.

By the way, as I am writing this, I am looking at a book with an intriguing title of "*Just sit there and do nothing*" (As opposed to the usual saying of don't just sit there. Do something.)

This book's Buddhist author, Sylvia Boorstein, reminds readers that meditation on a cushion and just being with what unfolds, is a skillful way to live. In the Japanese Zen tradition just sitting and staying open to what arises is called Shikantaza.

> Shikantaza. I suspect that these Zen masters knew thousands of years ago, long before science "discovered" the truth that we get our best ideas when we do nothing and just sit.

I suspect that these Zen masters knew thousands of years ago, long before science "discovered" the truth that we get our best ideas when we do nothing and just sit. I love doing that in a steam shower after a long run outside. It is what I call a good sit.

Both sitting and moving are happiness boosters. When we balance the two, applying equal effort, we experience what Thomas Carlyle observed: "Silence is the element in which great things fashion themselves."

Maybe I will get better at doing *both* sitting in Shikantaza and running like the wind—in a balanced manner. Like the black and white Yin Yang symbol there must be a fine and exact balance.

In addition, I am now making the time to purposefully move throughout the day, even after a long run at dawn. I move even if only for a few seconds at least once every 20 minutes--except when asleep on the couch after dinner!

As the band, The Byrds, used to say (and I am paraphrasing) in their famous song *Turn! Turn! Turn!*", there is indeed a time for everything, a time to sit and a time to run. Be wise and do both. Never allow your morning exercise routine to delude you into complacency.

- **Sit, but not too long and move, but not too much. Stay in balance.**

THE HEART

Not so long ago I heard a story about NASA monitoring the heart rates of astronauts. During the Apollo series, NASA knew *exactly* the various heart rates of these amazing human beings, strapped to a rocket carrying plenty of fuel, ready to explode upon take off. I was told the amount of fuel burned off in 20 minutes at lift off equals the volume of an Olympic-sized swimming pool.

Apollo 11 was just about ready to launch and two out of the three astronauts on board had heart rates way over 130. One had a heart rate of only 80 beats per minute. Buzz Aldrin was cool and calm. Aldrin was completely un-phased by what was going to happen next.

Some observers said it shows that in any situation we use our attitude to control what happens next. But is it always true that our heart rates are controlled more by our attitudes than our environment? The inside determines the outside.

I was not born in Canada, but this country became my new home in the early 1980's. Most people think of Canada as an extremely cold county. It is very true indeed. But it is also true that for a very, very brief season it can be extremely hot.

I discovered this one summer's night in Edmonton. Once again, my running taught me how to navigate life itself.

Out of over 100 marathons this was the only one which started at 5 PM. Sunset in a city that far north of the Equator can be as late as 10 PM. The goal of this race, as the organizer promoted it, was to finish before sunset.

At the start my heart rate was far higher than usual. I attributed it to a false reading. Perhaps I was picking up the reading of my neighbor? (In those days, technology was a bit iffy—not as advanced as it is currently.)

As the race unfolded, I discovered that my heart rate monitor was in fact correct. Due to the heat—which **increased** as we got closer to 10 PM—my heart was beating way faster than usual.

It ended badly. Perhaps the worst ever out of 100 marathons. With about one mile to go I had to find a bush to hide behind while I emptied my stomach. (My bladder emptied 24 hours later due to a miscalculation of my hydration and besides…I could not keep fluid down long enough for it to get absorbed.)

I learned a very valuable life lesson that day—one which is true for all of us.

Listen to your heart.

Physically heart rate monitors rarely lie, but metaphysically the heart may lie.

Many New Thought teachers teach that we should listen to our hearts. Listen to your intuition or core they encourage their followers. You already know what you need to know; ignore gurus; listen to the guru inside. Follow your heart.

Everything in life must be cultivated over time. So, my question is how did you cultivate your heart? How did you guard it daily? Scriptures encourage us to do it consistently because it determines the *entire* course of your life. (Proverbs 4:23)

As a holistic life coach and physician, I have discovered that the heart and mind are closely interconnected. The harmonious functioning of the heart and mind increases our energy. By cultivating Na'au, a Hawaiian word for the unification of the mind and heart, we are better able to trust our heart.

It is good advice to listen to one's heart, but make sure it is a well-cultivated heart. Restore your core first. Train it like you train your body and your mind. After all, the heart determines your thoughts, views, actions, words, and overall fitness. Almost like the first button of a shirt controls all the other buttons that follow. Make a mistake with the first button and all subsequent buttons are wrong too.

Marathon running taught me one thing for sure: the heart never lies. It is like a black box in a passenger jet.

- **Pay attention to the state of your heart, but also make sure you cultivate a wise heart before you trust it.**

CHEMICAL CASCADES

As a physician I will always be fascinated by the brain. It is still one of the organs in the body where we are the most limited in our knowledge of how it functions. The mysterious mind always seems to be just that—a mystery never to be conquered. It seems there are no ceilings or finish lines. The many ways in which the brain functions continue to surprise *even* experts and many of these ways seem to be immeasurable.

Can we measure what happens to the brain when we move?

When we exercise, we squirt and flush around neurochemicals all over the brain. That vital organ gets flooded with something called BDNF (Brain-Derived Neurotropic Factor). John Rattey who wrote "Spark", a book on how exercise benefits the brain, calls it "fertilizer to the brain." I will add that this fertilizer has nothing to do with smelly brown material, but instead it sets the stage for healthy living —*way longer* than if you allow stress hormones to flood your brain and damage it in the process.

> When we engage in activities that bring pleasure, chemical cascades flood our brains. These fertilizers work hard.

When we engage in activities that bring pleasure, chemical cascades of these good messengers flood our brains. If one were to run a functional MRI it will show that certain parts of the brain light up like a Christmas tree or Times Square in New York City on New Year's Eve.

But it is not only running that causes a flow state; a peak state as some researchers prefer to call it. There are other ways to create great chemical cascades.

Recently in my reading of medical journals I stumbled upon an article which described how the brain changes when we kiss our most loved companions. It caused a very brief cascade of good chemicals.

I believe Einstein may have said if you kiss your lover while driving you are not kissing him or her mindfully.

If you are not into running, that is fine...try kissing your partner often and do it for at least six seconds as some experts suggest. This "exercise" sets off a cascade of chemicals too.

- **Make it a point to fertilize your brain daily and do it purposefully and with joy.**

CROSS TRAIN

How many times have we read, "Everything in moderation"? But what does this mean?

I think a statement like this can sound great, but once one takes a deeper dive, one soon realizes that the sentence is incomplete. I have learned to put every common expression under the microscope. Trust but verify.

A better way to state things could be, "Everything in moderation, depending on the context of the situation."

My own story of running over 100 marathons may illustrate what I mean. I completed the goal of reaching 100 marathons by age 60—injury free. I never had to consult with any clinicians. It was only around marathon 104 that I realized my time had come. My time to be a patient. And sadly, I caused my own troubles.

For decades, my training was always marked by moderation. Nothing bad happened. I almost took a sense of pride in the fact that moderation paid off. Until the wild week when the wheels came off the wagon.

A few years ago, serious back issues slowed me down and it impacted me profoundly. (In fact, I mention it elsewhere in this book simply to underscore how this problem almost derailed my running career.) It arrived from seemingly nowhere. Experts looked and after visiting six experts...I ended up with seven opinions. The one I liked the least was this: "Stop running."

This was frankly quite absurd and *certainly* not helpful. Given my wiring, this was not an option. It would have been easier to convince the Pope to get married. I was not convinced that ending an activity which brought me so much energy was the way to go. My heart told me to consider things a bit deeper. I hit the pause button and started my own inner investigation. It was time to apply what the Buddha taught 2,600 years ago: see wisely and be attentive.

My research led me to discover Medical Therapeutic Yoga. I thus discovered the other side of a coin: *moderation may have a purpose to ensure you can sustain your primary purpose.*

It was indeed true that by training wisely and in moderation I was able to run injury-free for decades. But even so it was also important to supplement running with stretching and strengthening activities. Yoga provided me with, as the root-meaning of the word tells us, a sense of union or oneness. In this case moderation meant balancing various activities and seeing how interconnected these activities are. Although separate, all exercise is in the end one.

The word yoga is rooted in union (oneness). The whole body should be one rather than just various parts put together.

My injury became a gift. It was not hard to reframe my "setback" as an opportunity to learn more about holistic wellness. This story showed me what it means to reframe failure as success.

> My pain became my teacher.

The theme of one of Dr. Wayne Dyer's last books he wrote before he passed on, had to do with the fact that all people and events in this lifetime arrive in our sphere, not by accident but on purpose. When we look back, we can see clearly—if we have the right perceptions and the open-mindedness to always learn and grow.

As the title of Dr. Dyer's book, *I Can See Clearly Now* reminds us…what we may see as suffering, may be an opportunity to grow.

My pain became my teacher. And the teacher arrived at exactly the right time—when I, the student, was more than ready. I was ready to see the value of cross training, not just in exercise, but in life itself. In my case the discovery of yoga was God-sent.

- **All of us are really in some form of training if we are alive. To sustain a certain pace of living, remember the value of cross training.**

COOPERIZED

In the early 1990's I got Cooperized, but as you read this sentence, I am guessing you do not yet know what is involved in getting Cooperized...

If one were to use this word while playing Scrabble, I am unsure if it would be allowed as a legitimate word—would an opponent allow one to use it? Is it in the dictionary? Rest assured that word is legitimate. Use it.

I do not know if you may play Scrabble, but if you do, remember you read it here first.

Getting Cooperized is really very simple: one becomes a follower of the work of Dr. Ken Cooper also known as the father of aerobics. In fact, he was the first person who coined that word. Dr. Cooper is the founder of the Cooper Clinic in Dallas, Texas.

> The building may have been small, but Cooper's mind and heart for what he set out to accomplish was, as they say in Texas, bigger and better than anywhere else.

This clinic was started in 1970 by Cooper after he left the US Air Force. Driven by his enthusiasm to start a clinic where the health benefits of regular exercise and lifestyle medicine would become apparent, Cooper started in a small building located in a Dallas suburb. The building may have been small, but Cooper's mind and heart for what he set out to accomplish was, as they say in Texas, bigger and better.

Today the Cooper Clinic, sprawls over acres of land, dotted by huge stretches of green grass, Colonial style buildings and ponds and streams of running water. It attracts millions of visitors and patients from all over the globe. It has contributed immensely, not only to extending lifespans, but also healthspans. (Healthspan refers to not merely living into a ripe old age, but to also enjoying a healthy quality of living right up to the day of dying.)

Dr. Cooper at the time I type these words is still alive. When I think of him, I think of a man who lived a life by example. He did it daily. He sustained it and inspired millions around the globe to do the same.

One of the best things I believe that can happen to any human being is to be born—it took one out of a million sperms to fertilize one ovum— and you were that sperm who won! But as the saying goes there are two important dates in anyone's life: the day you were born and the day you found out why.

I sense Dr. Cooper knows why he was born.

One of the most popular books ever written is *The Purpose Driven Life.* Rick Warren, the author had no idea at the time of publishing this key book what an impact it would have globally. Being a humble man and a pastor of one of the biggest churches on the planet he gives all the credit to God.

The book's success may be Divinely inspired, but I also believe it has a lot to do with a basic human need to live life on purpose—people with no interest in the Divine yearn to find the true meaning of their lives.

Not all of us leave a public legacy like Warren and Cooper, yet we can leave a legacy even in a small manner within our family or our community.

One way to maintain a legacy is to share your knowledge. This is one way to achieve success. This is what I see when I read about what it means to be truly helpful.

Whatever your unique legacy may be, make sure it passes the test of time. You may not be keen on being Cooperized yourself but be true and stay true to your own calling and your own life by example. Share your knowledge. Not just for your own sake, but for generations yet to be born.

- **Role models must pass the test of time. The father of aerobics, and one of the reasons I exercise daily, passed his test of time with flying colors.**

DOES YOUR PALATE DO A HAPPY DANCE?

In decades of my work as a medical doctor I have observed that when it comes to eating healthy, too many of us are like a bird in a cage where the cage door is opened, yet we do not fly to liberty. Instead of pivoting to consistently consuming more nutritionally sound and healthy foods, we make all kinds of excuses to continue our bad habits; habits that make us feel trapped when in fact we are free.

Yet, just like gravity could not care less about what we believe about it, so nature does not care if we are sincere, but continue to eat junk food. It goes to work regardless of our beliefs and in the end, we reap what we sow. Many get fat and as we follow the SAD (Standard American Diet) diet, we cut off six years of our lifespan.

I used to be on morning TV segments for two decades. I remember one morning I arrived at the studio, bright and early, and met another guest who was there to talk about his book. He said something I shall never forget when I asked him about his views on human behaviour.

He said with a wistful voice, "When we know the things we know, why do we do the things we do?"

That was a very deep and valid question—one which I am frequently reminded of when I see the result of poor lifestyle choices made by millions. In fact, this is always the first question that pops up in my mind like toast pops up out of a toaster, when I read about 80% of patients in hospitals being there primarily because of poor nutritional habits. What were they thinking?

I listen to a lot of podcasts every week—commuting in heavy traffic, flying somewhere, and of course during some of my very long three to four hour runs. It is my way to stay current with the latest on science and nutrition.

Not so long ago I learned that the biggest killer in North America used to be cigarettes, but that is no longer the case. Having finished medical school in 1979 when we were taught how to help people quit the smoking habit, I wondered if current medical schools also teach students how to prevent the biggest killer at this time.

Sadly…they do not teach much at all about food. In fact, most medical schools teach almost nothing on this subject. Poor nutrition today kills more people compared to cigarettes, but unlike cigarettes, it is a slow insidious death. Most people are squeezed, like being in the grip of a python, by the consequences of their poor choices, and as soon as there is a momentary pause, they change from good habits back to the default of bad habits.

Some palates may do happy dances, savoring the unhealthiest and yet best tasting foods out there, but this comes at a great cost to society.

Very often I am asked in my talks and during television interviews on morning shows, "How do you fuel your body during your training and during marathons?" It is quite simple. My nutrition coach does not know me directly, but his pure common-sense approach remains the mainstay of what I do.

Michael Pollan, the author of the New York Times bestseller, *In Defense of Food*, told his audience that we should "Eat food. Not too much. Mostly Plants." Pollan's mantra has become mine. It is simple; it is true. It is also practical and realistic. And since I refuse to carry guilt, when I eat a healthy vegan meal it frees me from any second guessing or haunting guilt.

One can only imagine the expression on my great grandfather's face if I told him to eat real food. Like a curious dog, he would probably have tilted his head to one side; perhaps one eyebrow would go up; perhaps a frown would wrinkle his forehead. Real food, I tell patients, is food that rots—very simple. No need to apply rocket science here.

When I am mischievous, I tell my young patients to buy a hamburger from a famous drive-through restaurant and then simply leave it in a far corner somewhere in their home. A year later that burger still looks pristine. Untouched and perfectly "new."

There are several famous endurance athletes who are vegan. I have tried several times to be a 100% vegan or plant-based eater, avoiding all dairy and animal products, but the best I could do over a few decades was to be *predominantly* plant-based, until a year ago when I pivoted to whole-food plant-based nutrition only.

For those who are more disciplined, I highly recommend a superb resource based out of Washington D.C. called the Physicians Committee for Responsible Medicine. Their podcast, *The Exam Room,* and their website www.pcrm.org have resonated with millions of palates that did the happy dance, but so did the rest of their bodies. The evidence is overwhelmingly positive.

As athletes we are always looking for the best way to fuel our bodies. Food, religion, and politics seem to have lots in common—many cooks in the kitchen and people with passionate beliefs and yet far too often full of contradictions. That is why any information which is fact-based, and which leans heavily into research attracts my attention as a physician. One such a site where many papers are all archived in a single resource is www. nutritionfacts.org. Dr. Michael Greger and his staff do an amazing job of combing through the nutritional research and summarizing the current findings.

At the time of this writing more and more lay people have decided to become vegan. More and more doctors promote this lifestyle. Dr. Kim Williams, a former President of the American Heart Association, became vegan when he decided to deal wisely with his own cardiac risk factors. The American College of Lifestyle Medicine recently honored Dr. Dean Ornish, a pioneer in showing it is possible to reverse heart disease. Science, often respected for being objective and neutral, is very clear about this lesson I only learned in the twilight of my career:

- **Incorporate more plant-based foods daily and if possible, see for yourself if you can be a full-time vegan.**

WHAT THE CRUISE SHIP TAUGHT ME

I erroneously always bought into the narrative that cruise ships are mainly for older people who are retired, for people who like to eat as much as possible, or for youth who like to get drunk often and party till dawn. How wrong I was!

I shall always remember the time we boarded a ship in the Caribbean, after a fun day of onshore excursions. It was about to set sail. I realized that there were only six hours left before the day was done and I had not yet done my daily run. My streak was at risk. It was time to lace up my running shoes.

That run I did at sunset, on the top deck, sticking to my lane on an official running track, hearing steel drums, enjoying a windless and comfortably warm dusk, smelling the food being prepared for dinner as the sun was setting in the West, will stay with me for as long as I am alive.

After the run, as I watched the sun setting, I had no problem at all to just sit and be with what was—enjoying the moment fully and inscribing in my memory that incredibly special run.

My exercise was, as usual, one of the highlights of my day. Yet as much as exercise is discussed as way to lose weight—and as much as I am a keen believer in daily physical activity—I can tell you with great confidence, as a doctor with four decades of experience, that it is utter nonsense to rely only on exercise to keep one's weight under control.

What we eat matters way more than how active we are. It is so vital to know this truth that I must repeat it: *What we eat matters way more than how active we are.*

The sweat running down your forehead is not the leakage of extra calories.

I love watching the Oscars beamed from sunny, warm LA to our home in Canada, usually in the dead of winter. There is an Oscar for the main actor and one for the supporting actor or actress.

Let me make it simple. When it comes to weight management, the role of exercise will never win an Oscar for the main actor or actress; at best it can only expect to get recognition for a *supporting* role.

I ran every day and some days I ran really heard with a heart rate monitor telling me I was close to my maximum heart rate for my age. And yet I *gained* weight.

So, when I meet my obese patients, I look them in the eyes and tell them the truth:

- **Pay close attention to what you eat: way more than the daily steps you take**

MIND

Results follow action like a shadow.

The Buddha

Of all the many things that people value and care for in the world the mind is the most precious. In fact, the mind is the foremost treasure in the whole world. So be sure to look after it well. The mind is a priceless possession that should never be overlooked.

Ajahn Mun (Thai Forest Buddhist monk)

Know your mind just as it is.

Ryōkan Taigu, Sōtō Zen Buddhist 1758--1831

PSYCOPENIA

After all these years of running daily and doing a few marathons every year I can honestly say that it helped me to avoid psychopenia.

Soft bones are called osteopenia by doctors. In medicine if a word ends with *penia,* it refers to not enough.

Psychopenia refers to a mind that is weak, soft and on the verge of breaking. I prefer to call it mental vulnerability. Psychopenia is simply like being in a cold place and being vulnerable to the elements. Without a cozy, warm coat one can perish from exposure. Mental vulnerability can be deadly; usually the path to the bottom is insidious, protracted, and non-linear... until the sad end arrives one day.

Psychopenia and mental overwhelm cause disease one day at a time if left unattended. If unaddressed, mental flameouts result. Do not risk it! Instead become a member of the resilience gym.

I have observed that the most resilient people—those who joined the resilience gym—are the ones who developed a tool to help them organize their minds skillfully. They do it consistently. Their minds never get flabby like the flabby muscles of a lazy person.

I am reminded of Benjamin Franklin who taught us that if we pick 13 qualities we want to develop, it is a good idea to focus on one a week for 13 weeks and then to repeat the cycle three times over the course of a year for a total of 52 weeks. Franklin's list of 13 mental skills to develop included: gratitude; positive speech; tranquility; righteousness; gentleness;

respect for others; physical health; productivity; resolution; order; frugality; truthfulness; and humility.

Resilient people never shy away from asking difficult questions. They know by doing that they sometimes discover marvelous answers. In the Japanese Zen tradition, a beginner's mind is known as Soshin. A Soshin mind never stops learning. Its curiosity knows no bounds.

Mindfulness and insight meditation help us to see accurately and clearly. It is never too late to learn these skills. Meditation does not resonate with everyone. Others who belong to the resilience gym use prayer; some are just naturally programmed to be resilient and tough it out.

As for me? When I run, I am mentally stronger. It is just that simple. It is one of the main reasons I love to run. I honestly have never engaged in this form of wellness out of guilt and obligation. It is not so much about the running as it is about the *positive* side-effects of exercise.

There are many definitions of what it means to be in the flow or the zone. Scientists always find a way to complicate the simple. I like the simple approach and thus when I say I am in the zone I find I am in a place in time where I have no desire to be anywhere else at that moment.

- **Every mind needs to go to the mental gym. Find a mental coach to initiate training and then consistently cultivate resilience.**

UNIVERSITY OF SPORT

At the exact time I typed these words, history unfolded. Never in the history of sports did the two things you are about to read happen in two days.

One night the St Louis Blues beat the Boston Bruins to clinch the NHL championship for the first time in over 50 years. A few months prior to their victory night they were dead last. But somehow, they won. From rock bottom all the way to the penthouse in six months.

The next night the Toronto Raptors became the first ever non-USA-located team to win the World Championship trophy named after Larry O'Brien. Underdogs written off by many became the top dogs in the end.

Basketball was invented by a Canadian and finally a Canadian team won, although my wife's smart cardiologist pointed out that "Our Americans beat their Americans". In all fairness…Toronto is one of the most diverse major cities on the planet and the Raptors were made up of mostly Americans, but also players from Africa, Spain, and Taiwan. Journalists felt that Toronto put the world in World Champions.

Over the years of running, I discovered there are many lessons that The University of Sports can teach me. All sports are interconnected. By that I mean there are common lessons to be learned.

To illustrate the concept of interconnectedness, imagine a young man in Canada who was diagnosed with a condition known as osteosarcoma. It is a type of cancer of the bone and treatment may involve amputation.

Such was the fate of this young man. Did he quit? Not at all. Instead, he chose to run across Canada and raise funds for cancer research. His quest lasted 143 days and 5373 kilometers, until it became clear that his cancer had recurred. His run started on April 12, 1980 and ended painfully on September 1, 1980. His inspiring mental tenacity sustained him to the very end.

On June 28, 1981 he passed away at the age of 22.

> The mindset of athletes matters a great deal.

Today in many countries around the globe, there is a charity run known as the Terry Fox Run, named after this famous Canadian youth. Terry's mindset caused a ripple globally. Every wave in any ocean on this great planet remains not apart, but a part of the ocean. To this day these Terry Fox Runs raise millions of dollars to support cancer research.

To me one of the top lessons is that the mindset of athletes matters a great deal. So often we read about a star player on the team who waited until the very last seconds of a championship game to execute his or her best effort.

Think of a kicker in football who launches a kick from an improbable distance and in slow motion the opposing team watches the ball fly high between the two uprights of the goal posts. Think of a basketball launched from the big hands of a tall player with about two seconds left in the game...in slow motion one can see the arc of the ball as perfect...it lands on the rim of the net and bounces, bounces, bounces, bounces before it goes in and causes spectators to be on their feet and players on the floor—crying either from joy or frustration.

Afterwards the player calmly but confidently admits, "As soon as the ball left my hands, I knew it was the winning shot." Many famous players go on and deliver keynote speeches on how to never even *entertain* the possibility of failure. Not for a second.

Running daily for decades and reaching the finish line of over 100 marathons has a lot to do with one's thoughts. I think the famous baseball player and philosopher, Yogi Berra said, "Baseball is 90% mental, and the other half is physical."

I have found it to be absolutely true. As we know, truth is that which never changes. It never changes when one runs long distances. At some point it's mostly mental and the physical part, though important, fades into the background.

It is also true that what our minds dwell on are the seeds we choose to water.

So when I did another key marathon a while ago—I have forgotten exactly which one it was—it was my fourth attempt to run fast enough to reach Boston again.

It did not happen. I had to accept that even my best was not enough. It was not going to be for now.

Yet setbacks can at times teach us how a lemon becomes lemonade: It gave me an idea for my first book titled *Moving Forward*. Even though I did not reach my goal of qualifying for Boston, I was not a quitter. I could still keep moving forward.

Ever since that "bad luck" day I have moved forward and watered the seeds of positive thoughts even when most people would see the negative which was glaringly obvious at the time of my disappointment.

Watching important playoff games since then continues to teach me this:

- **Yogi Berra was 100% correct: 90% of my success so far has been all mental. To the degree I remember this, I can endure toward the finish line.**

DIG DEEP

One of the men in a men's group I belong to once told me a story of how he unexpectedly got caught in a blizzard. He was sure he was going to die. It was in the far north of Canada—an extremely remote area. There was little back-up support. It was all up to my dear friend, Sam.

Once Sam looked at a picture of his family, he was inspired to survive by digging deeper. All of a sudden he was all in; he leaned into the experience rather than fear it and, instead of imagining the worst possible outcome, he reframed it as a great opportunity to prevail for the sake of his beloved family. Many obituaries mention how so-and-so was fond of their family. Sam takes the love of family to a *much higher* level.

The most common spot to learn about digging deeper happens between 20 to 26 miles into a marathon. At 20 miles one is not yet close to being finished or almost there, and certainly not yet able to see the finish line.

Mile 20 is the spot in the marathon where the boys get separated from the men. My apologies to female runners—the same is true for them. They too need to dig deep at mile 20.

You see at mile 20 the race *only begins*. Most people can run 20 miles if they train properly. The big unknown is what will you feel like beyond that point.

And so it is with life itself. We do what we can, expecting it will help us get to the finish line, but at mile 20, a few miles short of the finish line, we discover troubles, set-backs, obstacles, hindrances, unsatisfactoriness—a moment where life gives us what we did not want or did not choose. And certainly not what we deserve or can explain.

It simply is so. Call it destiny; call it fate. It is so. We wish for it to be otherwise and wonder what we could have done differently to create a better outcome.

If we listen to famous faith preachers and respected new age gurus, we will soon believe *we alone* control almost all of life. Both require a deep degree of trust with no final proof; simply a surrender to trusting. Some may even see such beliefs as bordering on the delusional.

The good news is that we do not control as much as we think or believe we do. We only have limited control at best. The terrific news is that we *do* control how deep we want to dig in.

Sometimes we may train hard and hit the wall. Sometimes we train less than we should, and for reasons not known to the ordinary man or woman, we feel good at mile 20 and push forward by digging deeper and crossing the finish line with no drama at all.

Another marathon had this sign which I always recall when I hit proverbial walls:

- **When you hit the wall...demolish it.**

SAILS

I recently rounded a corner not too far from where I live and saw sailboats on a lake. Just another day and another familiar sight.

The night before, I read that it is not the wind that determines the direction of sailboats, but rather the way the sails are set. Even more surprisingly—as if to reassure me just a little bit more—a few days after I spotted the sail boats, I read a book on resilience and discovered these words written by William Arthur Ward: *The pessimist complains about the wind; the optimist expects it to change; the realist adjusts the sails.*

> And so it is with the way we respond to what happens to us.

And so it is with the way we respond to what happens to us. I have been guilty of blaming the wind, while it is really my choice to change the setting of the sails.

Another thought crossed my mind as I continued my morning run: who provides the wind and whose job is it to set the sails? Personally, I trust in a Higher Power. Higher meaning a Force that is beyond my comprehension. A Force that may just explain why my nails grow at night when I sleep—regardless of my beliefs—or why a rose opens the way it does, or the sun rises exactly on time during both the shortest and longest days of the year and in between.

A Sufi poet calls this Force, "the breath within my breath." Tolstoy said, "To know God is to live."

The day after I first read that, was the day I started to utter a moment of gratitude before every run—gratitude for lungs to serve me for decades of running daily and covering close to 3,000 kilometers every year the past thirty years.

As a holistic life coach, I teach clients that we co-create with our Creator. It is not our job to determine the speed or direction of the winds, but it is our job to hoist the sails if we want to move forward. That to me is the main reason I prefer a realistic approach to life's events—rather than being like the pessimist who complains about the wind or the optimist who believes his or her faith will make the wind go away.

Trying to stop the wind is delusional—it only adds to suffering.

One of my favorite musicians is Paul Simon. Not so long ago I was thrown around by a strong wind which came out of nowhere during an evening run.

The words "Who am I to blow against the wind?" rang in my ears. These are the words from a Simon song inspired by music he heard in South Africa, the country where I was born. The title of the song is "I Know What I Know."

Over the years of running I know what I know. What I know is this: resist the temptation to try and blow against the wind; some things must simply be accepted for what they are—especially the ones where we tend to forget we do not control anything. So surrender and experience equanimity, which is a stability of mind, regardless of circumstances.

In training daily for over a hundred marathons I had to do my part, but by Grace, I have been kept healthy and alive to reach the finish lines 100% of the time.

- **Next time you are upset when things do not work out, remember that you do not control it all. Blowing against the wind is a waste of energy.**

SUFFERING TWICE

I have a special book on suffering which I keep close to me where I work in my study. The book is titled, *Who Ordered this Truckload of Dung?*

This book, written by an Australian Buddhist monk, in a clever and witty manner, looks at the roots of our suffering, but also suggests timeless truths to put into use when aspiring to develop power over difficulties. Recently a very good friend of mine, Allan Donsky, a child psychiatrist, referred to difficulties as, "The yucky stuff."

In the Buddhist tradition there is a term called "the Second Arrow". I often think of that after I finish tough marathons—the ones where I miss my goal by a mile; the ones where I convince myself to try and count even one thing that went right when a thousand things went wrong; the one's where I aim to recalibrate to do *way* better next time; the ones where I remind myself to be with what was or is. It is so—it cannot be otherwise. One does not always control the weather or the number of hills along the way.

What is the second arrow?

> Imagine a bad situation and as if that were not bad enough…WE OURSELVES make it worse.

Imagine a bad situation and as if that were not bad enough…WE OURSELVES make it worse. *That* is a second arrow.

They say that if we all gather in one place and bring all of our troubles with us and then sit in a circle and throw all those troubles to the middle of the circle, many of us—the majority—will pick up our own troubles when asked to choose another problem from the circle.

The truth is we may suffer, but sometimes we alone—nobody else— make it worse.

Over many years as a physician, I have learned this truth: people with a horrible self-esteem may suffer lots; they often end up with huge egos trying to compensate for their low self-esteem; they are out to prove to the planet that after all they are very, very worthy.

They are driven; they try to fix the planet; they are often outliers and they become a royal pain in their own behinds—and ours too when the waves created by their choices start to make our own boats rock back and forth. Their self-centeredness becomes intolerable to many and they often end up lonely or frustrated. Some burn out. Some become famous for explaining how their driven nature burned them out.

In the running community there are sometimes people with huge egos. I often wonder if it is not an issue of low self-esteem. Maybe a titanic ego is a cry for help; a form of insecurity.

Sooner or later even big egos discover that to be excessively driven ultimately leads to suffering. Some learn the lessons they are meant to learn: *inner contentment arrives when we see clearly that our own egos cause us to suffer twice.*

A far better alternative is to wake up to the fact of two arrows.

Suffering is optional. Setbacks are not optional. How I respond to setbacks determine just how much I will suffer. I read how a former President in South Africa made up his mind on second arrows.

Nelson Mandela, the former President of South Africa, was in jail for a long time. but when he got out, he chose to forgive the people who put him in jail. In fact, the story is told he invited the wardens who looked after him in jail to the inauguration as the new and first black President of South Africa. When asked why he did that he explained, "If I did not forgive them, I would still be in jail."

So much has been written about forgiveness and it is probably one of the hardest things to do. In addition, one must forgive oneself. That is not mentioned as often as forgiving others.

Marathon running, and more importantly, marathon training, has taught me that there are plenty of opportunities to forgive oneself: not training hard enough; not listening to one's body, starting a run too fast, and being unable to sustain a certain pace; comparing oneself—almost in a delusional manner—with other runners who are way better, rather than running in a customized, authentic manner, even it means to run in a way slower lane.

The physical effort of running 26.2 miles, pales in comparison with the mental efforts it takes to run a life.

Try adjusting to losing a limb; losing a child; saying goodbye to a loved one who did not get proper medical care, because there was a viral pandemic… these are indeed yucky moments.

I call these chapters in our lives mental-marathoning and I always watch out for those second arrows; the ones we create on our own, because we get captivated by stories that really do not serve us well. We insist on believing them. When we cling to wrong stories, we suffer twice.

So, while moving forward after a grueling race I am always on the guard for this danger:

- **Watch out for the second arrows; dodge them…or better…do not fire them off toward yourself.**

DIALED IN

In the world of athletes there is a distinct vocabulary. To many athletes the words "dialed in" refer to being fully involved, committed and in the zone. It is when all cylinders fire together at maximum function, but still in an efficient and sustainable manner.

To be physically dialed in is the goal most athletes aspire to achieve along the path to reaching their full potential. To be caught up in this sweet spot is hard to capture in words. It is simply a knowing not many athletes experience consistently.

The other morning, I came back from a run where I was physically dialed in. Earlier that morning I woke up tired because of insomnia that kept me wide awake for most of the night.

Yet, being committed to daily workouts, "camping" under the covers was not an option. I went out and was dialed in 90% of the time only to arrive back home just when the sun rose above the horizon. I felt good. The bright orange skies to the east inspired me deeply. I felt connected to all of creation. My bulldog-mentality delivered big mental dividends.

I enjoyed every step along the stairway to the bathroom, ran some water into the sink and got out of the shower five minutes later, only to get jolted by stepping onto a soaking wet floor.

I forgot to pay attention.

Clearly, I forgot to pay attention—or as some teachers teach, I forgot to remember to remember. I was so excited that a run went well that I forgot to notice the next moment fully. There was no watchman over my mind as some would define the meaning of paying attention and being mindful.

Thankfully, it could have been worse were it not for a little hole.

The reason the sink did not overflow more was very clear to me: a small little hole in the sink drained some of the water. I wonder if that design was discovered and hopefully patented by a plumber who got one too many calls to come and fix messes by sinks which overflowed.

As I turned the faucet off, I admired that little hole with gratitude. The thought occurred to me that while I was dialed in physically, I forgot to pay attention. Had it not been for the small drain in the basin there would have been a major flood.

We all need reminders to have some outlets when there is overflow.

- **If we forget to pay attention to small things in life, they can add up and cause floods of troubles. Remember to remember.**

DEAD BODIES

Marathon running has taught me how to set goals and to be consistent in my efforts to reach them.

Recently I read about goals which were associated with dead bodies. The story taught me that although passion for a certain goal is often admired, one should not cling tightly to a goal which will destroy one in the end. To yearn with passion is good, but to grasp *too* tightly could possibly become deadly.

To scale the summit of the world's tallest mountain is the goal of an ever-increasing number of humans. So much so that a letter-writer in the morning paper delivered to my doorstep wondered if it is not time to limit the number of climbers, not just for the sake of ecology (protecting the fragile mountains) but also for the sake of safety.

In one week almost 18 people died trying to summit Mount Everest. A photo of climbers lining up while waiting to get to the top went viral on social media. Sadly, some climbers ran out of oxygen because of having to wait too long...and died. Other climbers had to climb over the dead bodies to get to the top.

Marriages die because of the high price of goals that some partners took on. I know of a man in his eighties, worth quite a few million dollars. He himself admits that to get there cost him two marriages. As a result, one of his biggest fears is that all the money that came at such a high price, may be squandered by others when he is gone.

Some athletes run through injuries, and like Navy Seals, are celebrated for their grit; others fail to listen to their bodies and run through injuries. That endurance event then becomes their last. They never compete again.

> Stubborn or determined? There is a fine line between the two options.

Stubborn or determined? There is a fine line between the two options. It is not for me to judge. As a doctor we ask many questions before we make a diagnosis. It is easy to make the wrong diagnosis when one does not have all the data.

All I can say is that each of us knows we already have a sensor inside of us. Not a sensor like a fitness tracker or some other sophisticated technological gadget of the day. Our sensor is as old as the hills. It is our hearts.

If your heart tells you the price of a goal is too high…then it probably is true for you. Always keep the price of your goals in perspective and aligned with both wisdom and compassion.

Don't fight the odds. Listen to the voice of wisdom, already placed inside of you for your own protection, and tune out the ego which so often pushes us further down the wrong path—the path of failure. Aspire to reach goals, but pace yourself wisely along the way.

- **While it is wise to set big goals, always remember each goal comes with a price. Don't overpay.**

THE CEMENT WALL WAS CRUEL

We all have heard it at least once: in sex, politics, and war it is all about timing. But in marathon running and in life itself, timing is what *it is all about*.

The pace runners choose to train at and then stick to on race day is symbolic of how we all pace ourselves by deciding what to take on in life and what to say no to.

Where I live the local marathon was once sponsored by a company that makes cement. They must have had a twisted sense of humor, because right at the 20 mile mark they built a wall next to the marathon route...a wall that stood out on purpose.

> Many "hit" a wall with about six miles still left to endure.

I have written before about how this wall can mess with marathon runners. It is worth mentioning it once more because it really is the essence of enduring in the race of life itself, so often marked by mental obstacles that at times require almost unbearable endurance.

Most people who have done at least a few marathons have noticed that one can run for quite a while and then suddenly, out of nowhere, hit the wall at around mile 20. Lactic acid builds up along the way and energy stores run low. Many "hit" a wall with about six miles still left to endure.

Yet if one uses wisdom in pacing oneself according to the pace that is customized, the risk of hitting the wall diminishes significantly.

There is no need to hit the wall figuratively speaking. Not in marathons and not in life.

- **Some walls are real, and others are imagined. Be wise to know the difference and prepare at the right pace.**

DOING OUR BEST

What would make a book resonate with millions of readers around the globe?

I read this book many years ago, but during a recent morning run a good friend of mine, Dr. Rob Cohen told me this book revolutionized his life. It inspired me to dust off my personal copy which I re-read in *one* day. It's an easy read and filled with timeless wisdom. The premise is very simple and specific.

This book, first published in 1997, and translated into 46 languages worldwide, has a title which creates curiosity for most who never heard of it before. The book is simply called: *The Four Agreements*.

The Four Agreements are as follows:

- Agreement one: Be Impeccable with your word.
- Agreement two: Don't take anything personally.
- Agreement three: Don't make assumptions.
- Agreement four: Always do your best.

After completing many marathons, I have experienced the fourth agreement many times: my race did not unfold as expected but at least I know that I always gave it my best effort. By Grace, I started 112 marathons and finished 112 marathons, because of this principle. And yes, my worst finish time will be kept a secret—at least I finished!

The simplicity of these Four Agreements seems to resonate with many. Yet the question can be asked "How do we sustain such a goal to always do our best and surrender the outcome to what that day may bring?"

It is done the same way one runs a long marathon—one step at a time. Or in the quest to endure life and arrive semi-intact at the finish line, one can say it requires a concentrated cultivation of sustaining day-by-day living.

In my study, where I have the daily ritual to meditate before setting off on a run, I keep a copy of a piece of writing which reminds me of the dailyness of life and our aspirations to always cultivate healthy attitudes. This list of wise habits was penned by Sibyl F. Partridge and is titled *"Just for Today."*

In doing my best, here are the words I try to live by, day-by-day and step-by-step:

*JUST FOR TODAY**

1. Just for today I will be happy..
2. Just for today I will try to adjust myself to what is.
3. Just for today I will take care of my body.
4. Just for today I will strengthen my mind.
5. Just for today I will exercise my soul in three ways.
6. Just for today I will be agreeable.
7. Just for today I will try and live through this day only, not to tackle my whole life

It is indeed simple but not easy to cultivate the great art of doing one's best and then surrendering the outcome to a Universe beyond our comprehension or control.

---

* For a full version of Just for Today, see www.sk-alanon.ca/pdfs/pamphlets/ M12 just for today.pdf

Looking back at all the lessons I learned over the past thirty years of running, and specifically the time since I decided to run every day of my life, I am fully convinced by this truth:

- **Always do your best and surrender the outcome to a Higher Power.**

THE SOUTHBEACH JESUS

I decided on December 16, 2009 to run every day for the rest of my life. At the time of writing these words, by the Grace of God, my running streak has remained alive.

As I mentioned before —a few times now to make the point of how I see it as a very important decision— I spend at least 30 minutes in what I call my sacred space after I rise every day. I have a study filled with amazingly powerful books and this room faces east.

It is here where I set daily intentions and listen to what speaks the loudest to my heart in that moment. Sometimes what I "receive" while being still is so good that I jot it down on a blank sheet I always keep next to me. Many of the ideas in *this* book came because of this habit of mine.

Not so long ago my thoughtful wife, who knows me better than anyone else on this planet, shared a video with me. I started my day, watching what I call "The man who has no passport." This story spoke very convincingly to me.

The man with no passport lives in Southern Florida and some call him the South Beach Jesus, because he resembles common images of Jesus Christ. His name is Robert Kraft, but he is known as Raven. Robert decided on January 1, 1975 to run eight miles every day and so far he has not missed a single day, running the same route on Miami Beach. Every day at 5:30 pm he starts at the same lifeguard station and follows the same path on the beach, either alone or with whoever shows up that day.

As a result of running daily, always aiming to learn new ideas and integrating holistic life coach principles in my work as a physician, I came up with the *Ten Principles of Moving Forward*:

- The essence of our life is guarding our hearts with all diligence.
- We are here to be truly helpful and to remain sensitive to the needs of others.
- Being kind and representing Him, who is love, is the essence of our being.
- By associating with the wise we become wise.
- We are inspired by others, but not intimidated by comparing and competing.
- The proper awareness of our identity, purpose and passions leads us to reaching our full potential.
- We intentionally cultivate resilience which allows us to never give up and finish the journey with a joyful heart.
- We choose self-compassion, not only for our own sake, but also for the sake of others.
- Forgiveness of others and ourselves is the only path to real freedom and inner peace.
- We can choose to make the most of the time we have. What we do with it is our gift back to the Creator.

One of those principles is to never compare oneself with others, but instead to run one's own race.

After I watched the inspiring story of Raven the Runner, I briefly felt inferior. Very quickly I caught myself and instead used one of the Ten Principles of Moving Forward where I wrote how important it is to not have our joy stolen by our factory-settings of comparing and competing far too often for our own good.

Comparison indeed is the thief of joy as Theodore Roosevelt once observed. Mark Twain went even further by writing that comparison leads to the *death* of joy. (Italics added by author)

Of course, we will not always hear that voice inside that speaks the loudest to us about the day ahead. But stay open—be willing to hear with open ears, an open heart and an open mind.

- **Stay open at the start of each day to the inner voice and deliberately guard against the two terrible thieves of joy—also known as comparing and competing.**

DIAMOND THOUGHTS

As a long-distance runner there are hours and hours when we get to think—sometimes alone and sometimes when we run with friends who make us think. My wife often tells me I am doomed to too much thinking. I think she may be right, but meanwhile I am trying to think less and less as I struggle to overcome my propensity toward thinking too much.

Our brain is an amazing organ. It is the biggest consumer of the body's energy, using approximately 20 to 25% of its oxygen and 60% of its glucose for the communication between neurons and cells. So often we forget to use it to its full potential by being aware, mindful, and in control of our thoughts and emotions rather than the other way around.

One of my mentors Dr. Jerry Jampolsky, taught me that our thoughts create our reality; that we get to choose our thoughts; that we should never think hurtful thoughts toward others or ourselves.

Scriptures teach that as we *think* in our hearts, so we *will be*. (Proverbs 23:7)

An influential author and teacher on the matter of cultivating the right thoughts, Dr. Norman Vincent Peale, coined the term, "The Power of Positive Thinking."

The book with that title sold millions of copies and remained at the top of the New York Times bestseller list for a record time. It still resonates to this day with millions of readers. I doubt it will ever go out of print. I keep a copy by my bedside for easy access, especially at key moments before I turn the lights out at bedtime.

When it comes to learning from interesting books on the matter of how we are to think skillfully, I recently discovered another ancient book of wisdom known as the Diamond Sutra.

The Diamond Sutra is one of the great and oldest spiritual texts. The Sutra raises four key questions.

The four questions to ask, according to the Diamond Sutra, when a thought enters our minds are:

- Is it true?
- Can I *absolutely* know that it's true?
- What happens when I *continue* to believe that thought?
- What would I be *without* that thought?

- **Your thoughts always precede an action. It is a forerunner. Cultivate diamond thoughts daily.**

START YOUR SINGULAR TRAINING

Not long ago I read a great book—all in the hour before my daily run. How did I manage to read it in one hour? It was an easy read because it was rather repetitive. It took close to 200 pages to make the same point over and over and over again: *focus on one thing only.*

Life is like a marathon—it certainly is not a 100 meter sprint, where in ten seconds or less, it is all over. Life requires singular focus year after year after year.

But even in preparing for a ten second sprint one must be singularly focused. I am always amazed at the number of humans on this planet who spend years and years preparing for a race which may last slightly less than ten seconds. The difference between the winner and the loser is usually miniscule—very often, all six finalists can be covered by a surface area the size of a blanket!

Whether it is marathon running or sprinting, one *must* start training for what lies ahead. Life itself is no different.

But what is meant by training? And what does singular look like?

We can be focused on one thing only such as externals; the body, the outside, the wrinkles, the grey hair, the fake hair, the makeup, the bank account, the private mansions with stunning views of oceans or mountains, the status we have in communities, and on and on—all externally driven.

We can choose to focus only on the externals and then get to meet those who are so heavenly minded they are no earthly good. For them, it is all about the spiritual existence. These people tell us we are not a body. We are a spirit having an earthly experience. We are just visiting this planet. There is no self. We are more than our bodies. This life we live is just a dream.

I find this very unrealistic; it is also extreme and hard to believe in. I understand the value of spirituality, but extreme statements that we are not bodies is a bit too one-sided for my own comfort.

When we visit Harvard, Yale or Stanford we will find dozens and dozens of highly educated folks who train daily to improve their minds and become better than the day before. It is all about the mind—logic; the brain; functional MRIs; the intellect; the evidence which drives science. Nothing else exists. Only our brains drive everything. The right brain (our abstract and creative side) is for weak "sissies", dreamers and delusional thinkers. The left brain is for winners. These kinds of human beings train only the brain—singularly focused on the mind and intentionally ignorant of spiritual matters.

I always remember that logic begins with the letter L and thus the left brain is the logical brain. The right brain is for right dreaming and right creating.

In my 40-year career as a doctor dealing intimately with real patient-related issues, and recently as a holistic life coach…I am absolutely convinced that:

Balance is key

So, when you prepare and train for what lies ahead, remember two things: yin and yang.

Even the Creator teaches me that there is indeed a God who is all loving, but there is also a God who creates evil according to Scriptures (Isaiah 45:7); a God who judges; a God who may be easily misunderstood as being unloving and mean.

Two sides indeed. Yin and Yang. Dark and light.

The day I finished reading the book before my daily run—a book whose premise was that in life there is only one thing—I realized that for me the one thing to remember daily is that life must be lived in a healthy, balanced manner.

In medical terminology we call it homeostasis. It refers to a body where everything is functioning as it should—not too much or too little; always in perfect balance.

- **When you prepare for the life ahead of you, remember that staying balanced along the way is a good practice to cultivate.**

99.99%

We all have sent an email which bounced back with a message that it could not be delivered. Usually, it is one single error. The email is usually 99.99% right. Only an extra L is missing for Michelle—we think its Michele, but it is not. Allan is spelled Alan, but we add an extra L.

We are good friends with a married couple named Allan and Michele. My smart wife reminded me to say that she gave one of her L's to him. Where would I be without my wife? But that is a topic for a future book.

One silly mistake—a minor, yet important one—makes an email delivery impossible and not good enough. Perfection alone works.

In my case, people often spell my last name Neiman, rather than Nieman which leads to emails not getting through…and then when they see me, they tell me "I sent you an email and you did not get back to me. You are usually quite prompt at responding."

Or a comma is hit on the keyboard, by error, in a moment of distraction; a small difference but big enough to cause the email to bounce back.

Not so long ago a thought popped up in my mind, like a gopher pops out of a hole. It was at a time when I planned my next marathon. I heard the words "Do your best and leave the rest."

But then it occurred to me that if my best does not include very long runs to get my mind and body programmed to endure for hours and hours, it will be like the 99.99% concept. Good but not good enough.

In preparing for marathons, and some harder chapters of our lives, we need a mindset that I refer to as "long-run-thinking". This takes deliberate dedication, courage and planning. Many times, we can only aspire to reach perfection. Our world is imperfect and so are we—we all are and always will be 99.99% ers in some way, shape or form.

Since we all are prone to be swayed back and forth by our emotions, it takes concentration and mindfulness to stay even minded when the going gets tough. A poem by Rudyard Kipling that I keep in a binder close to me in the study and read during my own moments of "mental-marathoning", reminds me of what it takes to stay even-minded and tranquil, regardless of what life dishes out to us.

IF

If you can keep your head when all about you
Are losing theirs and blaming it on you,
If you can trust yourself when all men doubt you,
But make allowances for their doubting too:
If you can wait and not be tired of waiting,
Or being lied about, don't deal in lies,
Or being hated, don't give way to hating,
And yet don't look too good, nor talk too wise:
If you can dream—and not make dreams your master;
If you can think— and not make thoughts your aim;
If you can meet with Triumph and Disaster
And treat those two imposters just the same;
If you can bear to hear the truth you've spoken
Twisted by knaves to make a trap for fools
Or watch the things you gave your life to, broken,
And stoop and build 'em up with worn-out tools;
If you can make one heap of all your winnings
And risk it on one turn of pitch-and-toss,
And lose, and start again at your beginnings
And never breathe a word about your loss;
If you can force your heart and nerve and sinew

To serve your turn long after they are gone,
And so hold on when there is nothing in you
Except the will which says to them: "Hold on!"
If you can talk with crowds and keep your virtue,
Or walk with Kings—nor lose the common touch,
If neither foes nor loving friends can hurt you,
If all men count with you, but none too much;
If you can fill the unforgiving minute
With sixty seconds' worth of distance run,
Yours is the Earth and everything that's in it,
And—which is more—you'll be a Man my son.

What this poem shows me is that we can aspire to be the best possible person in any situation and though it is true that some things in life require perfection, it is also true that the world we live in is imperfect. Thus we can at best only aspire to reach 100%. Realistically there are many times when we need to be happy with 99.99%. Accept this and you may experience inner peace; resist this and suffering is certain.

As I look back at some of the slower marathons, I completed I need to remind myself that I managed to finish each and every marathon I started—all by Grace—and that:

- **For each of us the details of our own 99.99% principle may vary. Be mindful and remember, above all, your own 99.99%.**

APPLE JUICE

This story is about how we look at life and how we perceive things. Cultivating clarity of vision will always be a critical habit to develop—like watering the right seeds to get the right crops.

I have several favorite authors whose books left indelible imprints on my mind. One of those authors is Wayne Dyer who wrote "When you change the way you look at things the things you look at change." Please close this book now and reflect on what that may mean to you *personally*. I pray that these words will haunt you for the rest of your life, because they are profound, and once clearly understood, they will determine your own sense of equanimity.

Another all-time favorite author who resonates with my being is a Zen monk from Vietnam, who at one point was residing in France. He was nominated for a Nobel Peace prize. Thich Nhat Hanh taught me how to run more mindfully and how to experience a deep inner peace, a sense of equanimity, and a balanced mind free from turmoil.

As one can anticipate, this Zen monk, also known as TNH, tends to keep things simple.

Here are some of TNH's simple insights—paraphrased to fit my style:

- Start every day right by smiling as soon as one wakes up. Start with half a smile even.
- Always stay attentive to everything; the breath especially, and each step. The latter is known as "walking meditation."

- Have an eye of compassion toward ALL living beings.
- Keep one's speech pure by asking if it is timely, helpful, kind, necessary, and true.
- See how we all are in some way, shape, or form connected. TNH calls it "Interbeing."
- Be grateful every day for even the smallest things we take for granted so easily.
- Consume food and drink and media skillfully. (How *that* resonates so deeply in a world preoccupied by the latest technology? I must admit 99.99% of parents of my patients tell me that first and last thing they do, admitting it is not very smart to do, when they go to bed and when they wake up, is to reach for their "smart" phones.)
- Always look for opportunities to look deeper and thus understand better. TNH taught me that to love another person properly is to understand them in terms of where they are at.

One day I saw in one of TNH's many books a story of apple juice. He shared a story about kids who visited his monastery in France. It was a hot day. He offered then some apple juice. It was natural juice so some of the pulp made the juice look a bit cloudy. One of the kids did not like the look of things and rejected the offer to have a sip.

Much later the pulp had the time to settle at the bottom. By now the juice was clear. The same kid came back and ended up enjoying the same, but less cloudy, juice.

TNH made the point that in life we must allow for things to settle down so we can see clearly.

This is what I remember after some of my long runs when I rehydrate and restore my carbohydrate sources with apple juice:

- **Wait for things to settle down and once that happens, try to see clearly.**

DO YOU PEE?

I have lived in the Houston of Canada for almost forty years. When I first arrived in Calgary, I saw bumper stickers which read, "Dear God, let us have an oil boom again and this time I promise I won't piss it away."

Meanwhile, subsequent oil booms were peed away. Monumentally so. What used to be the lifeblood of Alberta's economy is on a steep and relentless downward slippery slope.

Given the general antipathy toward the petroleum industry, some people very much doubt that the old times will ever be back again. Time will tell. In the end it will become a matter of whose priorities will prevail. The current trend indicates that more and more humans agree that fossil fuels are on the way out. Instead, new opportunities await to transition to cleaner sources of energy.

Peeing away the wealth created by oil booms in the past is just one form of peeing.

> Another form of peeing relates to how we make personal choices.

Another form of peeing relates to how we make personal choices when we are given ideal opportunities. Some of us intentionally pee away our ability in order to keep our power. Instead of keeping it and allowing it to flow though us like air through the hole of a flute, we give it away.

I am very guilty of that—despite being coached by one of the best know and well-loved life coaches on this planet, Alan Cohen, who trained me to be a life coach. Alan reminds his students all the time "Refuse to give your power away."

How do we give our power away?

I do it often in winter. Where I live it is not uncommon to get a whole month in the dead of winter of minus 30 Celsius—every day, non-stop. Relentlessly my body gets assaulted by an Arctic air mass from the North Pole that slams into our city and never knows when to leave. One feels the cold down to one's bones.

I am still learning that when I fuss over how hard it is to run daily in these adverse and hostile conditions, where one's skin freezes in less than one minute, and where ski goggles protect one's eyeballs. Instead of electing to give my power away, my attitude should not depend on my environment.

Similarly, we allow people who are in pain to cause us pain. As the saying goes…hurt people hurt people. We give our power away and see ourselves as victims, while all along we can exercise our option to be like eagles who rise to a higher altitude where the crows cannot fly.

We fuss over things we cannot control and allow those things to dominate our emotions.

Over many years I allowed my power to be given away—to be peed away so to speak.

Not so long ago I read these words, penned by the Buddhist sage Shantideva:

> *Why be unhappy about something*
> *If it can be remedied?*

And what is the use of being unhappy about something
If it cannot be remedied?

- **Stay in control of your own inner peace and happiness and do not allow people and circumstances to dictate your joy or steal your power.**

TODAY IS A NEW DAY FOR THE ONE AND ONLY YOU

On a perfect summer morning, I looked at the sparkling surface of a huge lake, glittering in the bright morning sunshine. My wife and I were in a remote part of Saskatchewan. I had a pleasant and refreshing 8 hour sleep. My resting heart rate was in the lower forties. As I laced up my Nikes, I purposefully paused to set an intention for the new day ahead of me.

My mantra at the start of every day is: *Take nothing for granted—ever.*

We all are blessed with opportunities every day, but one opportunity, the chance to decide and choose our state of mind, is often taken for granted. I have been guilty of taking things for granted far too often.

But today was different. I was not going to take my morning run for granted. This gift was not delivered by UPS or FedEx. It was a gift from the Divine. Some call it "The Universe" or a "Higher Intelligence" and that is a personal choice. My attitude is that every good and perfect gift comes from my Creator who is indeed a Higher Power directing things from above or elsewhere.

I prefer to call the Divine…my Source. I often refer to God as the Breath in my breath when I run. In some Jewish traditions, out of respect, the word for the Almighty is spelled G-D. In my lexicon I use the term God for an Unlimited Power far higher than the limited me. I like the verse in Scripture which teaches that every perfect gift comes from Above. This morning was indeed perfect for a run with my dear wife. It was truly a gift.

I once was interviewed on a podcast, The Conscious Pivot. The host Adam Markel always reminds his listeners at the end of every podcast to be grateful and to have a morning ritual. Adam's ritual is to say, "*I love my life.*" Then he goes on to take a deep breath and remind himself as he inhales.... somewhere on this planet there are many who exhale for the last time, while I am aware of my first inhale of the day. Rituals that serve as reminders are worth cultivating.

We were renting a clean, bright, and well-designed suite through Airbnb. The owners taught me a lesson they did not know about. As I looked around our stunning accommodation, I could not help but notice the attention to detail. Every square foot was designed and maintained by a precise, detail-focused mind. My wife and I were the beneficiaries. The owners were my teachers and as is so often the case we teach others without knowing we are doing that.

As we covered the first few miles in fresh air, soothed by warm sunshine, I knew that this brand-new day provided me with many choices. Yet I set a simple and specific intention: *pay attention to detail just for today.* Start small, but nevertheless start.

Not by accident—at least without my own planning-- the tune on my iPhone just happened to be Sting's famous song "A Brand-New Day."

The Buddha taught that:

> *For these very reasons that it is difficult for a turtle to insert its neck*
> *Into a yoke adrift upon the vast ocean,*
> *It is more difficult to attain the human state.*

The odds to be born are not that high and that makes us all winners. Why? Because all our lives start as a sperm—one single sperm out of millions—which was *the one and only sperm* penetrating an ovum. We beat out millions of other sperms and developed into an embryo. We progressed day by day in our mother's womb and ultimately became the fearfully and wonderfully made human beings that we are. Every day of our life is a gift, and we are clueless as to when it may end. To consider death is not morbid but rather wise for it reminds us that to waste time assuming we have many more days ahead may not be that wise.

This confluence of all these miraculous events makes *each one* of us a miracle.

Get up every morning and decide to make the most of every day. Do your best and leave the rest…to the Creator of the Universe or chance if you do not subscribe to the belief of a Creator.

Remember the words of one of my favorite poems, Desiderata:

And whether it is clear to you the Universe is unfolding as it should.

Simply trust.

Returning to our cozy cabin next to the lake I was reminded of the words of Rumi: "Let yourself be silently drawn by the strong pull of what you really love." I really love running in nature.

That, at least, was *something* I could control. It was my choice to be mindful of my perceptions.

We do not control as much as we think we do but, no doubt, we alone decide how our attitude will determine our altitude at the start of every brand-new day. Make the priorities you set wise and useful—not just for your own sake but for the sake of humankind. Create huge ripples starting with your unique you.

- **Each new day gives all of us the opportunity to choose mindfulness which simply is cultivating the skill to pay attention.**

FUTURE

Mark Twain once said it is difficult to make predictions—especially about the future.

It was a spectacularly beautiful day and just before the sun rose, a starting gun went off to set a sea of runners surging forward in a colorful, diverse unison.

In the Tour de France they call a pack of cyclists "the peloton". In running? I am unsure what a pack of runners is called. Maybe they are called by the Greek word spelled: r-u-n-n-e-r-s?

I found myself with over 20,000 other runners somewhere close to the southern tip of Africa. This was my first ever ultramarathon—56 kilometers stretched ahead. I was quite nervous, and yet I harbored a pleasant feeling of excitement.

The tough course—one of the most spectacular long-distance races on this planet-- was peppered with hills throughout.

The main reason why so many runners show up for this event is its scenery. Known as the Two Oceans Marathon, the first part of the course meanders along the Indian Ocean and then runners have to conquer hills to get to the last leg, which unfolds along the Atlantic Ocean.

> Cape Town, where I spent my years as a student in medical school, ranks with Rio and Sydney as one of the three most spectacular cities in the Southern Hemisphere.

Cape Town, where I spent my years as a student in medical school, ranks with Rio and Sydney as one of the three most spectacular cities in the Southern Hemisphere. I often miss this amazing city. It set me up for where I am today. It provided an initial foundation.

I trained hard for the Two Oceans, knowing it can be demanding—more than most other marathons. My coach predicted a finish time for me based on the numbers we discovered during training. Things such as heart rate at various speeds and the heart rate recovery after a hard workout *supposedly* predicted a decent, but average finish time.

My weight was perfect. My sleep was sound. My body was fueled as close to perfect as possible. I was only slightly apprehensive seconds before the start, but ready to stick to my pre-determined pace.

This was my one and only ultra-marathon and for that reason, I shall never forget the moment when I got to the 26.2 mile mark. It is a marathon distance, but in an ultramarathon it means nothing—it is just a number. Many more miles were waiting to be conquered.

With about four miles left my body told me, "no more." Even with favorable numbers during the training, my coach could not foresee this nasty moment.

Quitting became very tempting, but only for a few seconds. I was walking instead of running. I had to remind myself that even when predictions fell apart, I was still standing and *moving forward*. Moving forward indeed is what makes all the difference between victory or failure. Now was the time to rely on a Navy Seal equivalent mind. Being fully aware of what moving forward means in this context suddenly became my only option left.

After what felt like forever, I crossed the finish line on the campus of the University of Cape Town. As I rested on my back, feeling the soft green grass underneath my fatigued body, I saw some clouds above, slowly coming and going—arising and passing.

It was supposed to rain that day, but it never did. Once again weather forecasters, using sophisticated computer models, missed the mark—just like me missing the mark of finishing in a predicted time. It became a metaphor for life.

The Buddha taught "Do not dwell in the past. Do not dream of the future. Concentrate the mind on the present moment." Some would argue with those words and claim that meticulous planning for the future is what matters the most.

At that moment, right on my back, feeling the dampness of the green earth under my body, the last thing I cared about was my future. I was simply present; fully present; exceedingly glad for health and vitality and following my breath *exactly,* like mindfulness teachers teach us, using the breath as an anchor. These teachers always remind us to come back gently and patiently to our breath when our mind wants to take us down some rabbit hole somewhere else.

We are often spending way more time in the future, rather than being completely in the present moment. This habit hinders our ability to experience more moments of inner tranquility.

On the news there are always a huge number of experts predicting the economic prospects and political outcomes. I am thinking of a regular newspaper columnist who is well-respected and read nationally. He always, at the end of the year, looks back and with great wit and self-flagellation explains how his own predictions never manifested.

- **It is indeed difficult to make predictions about the future. So try to be here, now, more often**.

TOO MANY TOMORROWS

During a recent pre-run ritual of reading something inspirational I read about death.

A book on a shelf close by, written by Bronnie Ware, *The Top Five Regrets of the Dying*, caught my attention. It is a very powerful book because it teaches us what people tend to regret as they enter the last few weeks or days of their lives. Often, I re-read this book as a reminder of what really matters during this brief journey on earth.

Bronnie, a palliative care provider, saw some common, but independent patterns of regret. She observed these top five regrets:

- I wish I had the courage to live a life true to myself, not the life others expected of me.
- I wish I hadn't work so hard.
- I wish I had the courage to express my feelings.
- I wish I had stayed in touch with my friends.
- I wish I had let myself be happier.

This book inspired me to consider my own mortality carefully and honestly. This is not a morbid activity. It is wise.

There is a saying that wisdom is shown by its results.

> Wisdom is shown by its results

In fact, wisdom is essential if we want to live life abundantly and on purpose. By doing that on a regular basis we don't procrastinate about our dreams and passions by assuming we have many more tomorrows. Instead, we pause and set priorities which help us to live more purposefully.

We will look back one day, a day that is for sure to come, and instead of having regrets we aim to have hearts overflowing with gratitude for lives well lived.

Not so long ago one of my good friends, Gary, invited me to join him for a drive in his amazingly fast Ferrari. It was my first-ever opportunity to be propelled forward on a freeway in this close-to-perfect technological piece of art. I marvelled that smart souls in Italy made it possible for me and Gary to be enjoying such perfection as we navigated our way on remote roads meandering all over the Canadian Prairies against the backdrop of the stunning snow-covered Rockies.

If Gary were Jewish, I am sure he would be called a "mensch."

It was at a time where I was still on a steep learning curve on how to get used to the fact that our youngest son lost his brave battle with depression and elected to end his life. It is indeed very true that we assume we have many tomorrows when in fact, more often than we realize, there will be no tomorrow.

I very rarely do up my shoelaces before I head outdoors without using that as an opportunity to pause and pray a prayer of thanksgiving for the opportunity to enjoy nature, the thrill of movement, and the rhythm of running at a pace suitable for that day; a pace that is flexible and aligned with the particular energy and state of mind certain days may bring.

I maintain this habit of purposeful-living—similar to maintaining a fitness plan. I tend to do all my runs at a customized pace. So far it consistently serves me well and keeps me on track to live life purposefully.

- **Purposeful living is a daily habit. Our tomorrows will always be uncertain. Water seeds of gratitude today and forever.**

TIMING

During many of my runs I often reflect on key moments in my past.

When I was a kid, I took the bus to school some days. At first, I did not realize that when one pressed the button that rung a bell to alert the driver to stop, there was sometimes a protracted delay before the bell rang. After a few trips which lasted longer than I wanted or planned, because the bus passed the stop where I was supposed to get off, I learned quickly: one had to know where the buttons were and then press them at the perfect time, at the sweet spot segment of the trip—not too early and not too late. It made the bus stop when I decided I needed to get off.

And when I think of timing, that image has stuck with me. I define timing as knowing when the right buttons of wisdom and knowledge are to be pressed; when to get off the bus or when to stay on it.

> Endurance has taught me which buttons
> to press and which ones to ignore.

We all decide where we get on and off when it comes to our commitments. Sometimes when the going gets tough, some get off the proverbial bus. Endurance running taught me to know beforehand where the buttons are, so that I know when they need to be pushed or not. So often during the testing of our patience we feel like pushing a button that will make the bus we are on stop so we can get off. But we refuse to push them. We stay on board. We finish what we start.

Some days because of what I observe as a life coach and a physician, I wonder if some couples want to get off the proverbial bus too soon. I wonder if some runners quit too soon.

I have also read numerous books on the secrets of a happy marriage. In reading all these books I get philosophical. I always find myself looking for the one thing they all have in common. I noticed that the difference between marriages that fail and those that succeed can be boiled down to one thing: commitment. When couples are committed to one another it is comforting to know, especially during deep times of testing.

Running has helped me to manage stress. My faith—which is another way of saying my *absolute* trust in a Higher Power—has sustained me. That Power is at work even when we don't see it. My commitment to enduring to the end is based upon this belief.

- **To everything under the sun there is a perfect timing. Stay open and alert to recognizing the key moments.**

ENOUGH

I was chewing on this thought like a dog chews on a bone—determined to not rush the process.

I was wondering during a recent run…*When is enough, enough?*

So many times, after I completed marathon 100 people asked me this: "So…what are your next goals?"

Translated: "Are you going to run more marathons?"

The answer is I have no goal to do 200, 300 or to be in the Guinness Book of Records for whatever hundreds of marathons at age 80. 100 was my goal. To 100 I got…intact and protected by Grace.

Now my goal is to do as many marathons as the Creator allows me to do, but in a less deliberate manner.

> Greed and attachment cause all kinds of suffering.

I am far less driven now. Greed and attachment, as many of the ancient Eastern Traditions taught, cause all kinds of suffering. What we cling to as if our life depends on it can actually kill us—slowly or fast.

In all of us there is a deep and intense knowing of what enough already means. Tune in to that frequency. *Enough Already* is a fine book which I often suggest to those who feel that enough is elusive. I invite you to read that book thoughtfully. When you do, you will see why.

The Enough Already "channel" streams *only* songs that deal with enough already. Just bookmark this imaginary URL named "Enough Already" in order to quickly return to it when necessary.

I have observed how money can suck people in. A wise teacher once observed that when he read the newspaper, he noticed four themes: sex, sloth, silver and self. In all four of these areas, money seems to play a major role.

For many wealthy humans who are "intoxicated" by thoughts of making *one* more million, enough is *never* enough. The grip of greed refuses to let them go and they confidently cling back in return.

Running has taught me this: know what is your 'enough' and stick to only that. Don't get sucked into greed. Listen to your heart. Be who you are rather than what you think others want you to be.

Greed is a magnet—it attracts with a powerful energy. It can be mesmerizing. Greed also has a twin brother called "Delusion."

Many know that greed can suck them in really effortlessly. But they sheepishly admit that while they know what they know, they keep on doing what they are doing. They may even delude themselves by telling convincing stories void of reality.

When they rest their heads on pillows at night after exhausting days, they know all about those mesmerizing feelings of greed; they are at times aware of their inability to control an insatiable sense of wanting more. Forever they seem to be unsatisfied and hungry for more. There is no finish line in sight at all for those who never experience enough already.

Today I decided to skip the next marathon which I planned for a future time. Instead of asking "Is there another one I can do?" I am saying I would rather be in the now—right here. And by *right* here, I mean *this time* is perfect and 100% suitable for where I am at. Enough for now.

Instead, I slept in for an hour and enjoyed the amazing company of my dear and wise wife. Later we ran together—a mere five kilometers. That was enough for that day.

When I write about Enough Already I experienced it that very day.

But I still experienced a runner's high during this brief run. Endorphins and other hope molecules washed my brain. It was a form of mental shampooing. Leaves smelled good. Cool air gently touched my face. I looked at my best friend and my heart was beating at only 100 beats a minute, but it was beating in pure love. I visualized a stream of light from my heart to hers. This was MY zone— not THE zone…but my zone.

- **Know when enough is enough. Be fully present in the zone, aspiring to overflow with gratitude, trusting that the Universe is somehow providing in ways we shall never fully understand.**

FROZEN

In Canada where I live winter lasts twice as long as summer. At the time of writing this book I have endured almost 40 consecutive winters here.

Not so long ago I rediscovered how frozenness can be a very potent metaphor—especially when it comes to dealing with aversions. Far too often we allow aversions to put us through some degree of suffering. It is as if our steady productive flow states end up being stuck in frozenness because of something we have an aversion to.

I am not fond of running on icy surfaces. One always has to stay alert for hidden ice patches that can lead to falls which can end a running streak in seconds. After a while it is hard to relax.

Our home is situated close to a lake with a well-designed running path where most of the miles are dotted by my unique footprints. I tend to run there all year round—even during the dead of winter. Some people have called me crazy for doing that at my age.

Recently I ran on this path, but during a *perfect* summer's day, after one of the coldest February's ever since records were kept of the local temperatures and environmental conditions.

On this bright sunny morning in mid-summer, butterflies danced all around me. The smell of colorful lilacs filled the early morning air. A dozen ducks were floating on a mirror-like surface close to the edge of a huge lake and birds were chirping away, hidden in trees completely covered with lush, deep green leaves so thick one could not even see the branches. The air hung still for a while, but as the slight breeze hit me in my face turning a corner it felt good…I needed the soft balmy breeze on my perspiring body.

I entered our home after yet another invigorating run. Soothed by stunning scenes of nature and with my running streak still intact, I remembered how hard it is at times to navigate cold weather running.

In addition to actual frozen environmental conditions some of us also face frozen relationships with dear ones.

A parent of one of the families I provide medical care to in my clinic reminded me of another type of frozenness: frozen family relationships.

Sadly, the parents got divorced and on Father's Day the father noticed that all of his children froze him out—they rejected his calls and text messages. They wanted absolutely nothing to do with him. He blamed their mom and told me how unfair he felt that was.

I felt his sadness. He was frozen out and the rejection must have felt like being kicked out in the cold and left to fend for himself.

That was then, and my friend these days has managed to bounce back and move forward—one day at time. They say grief is something we never get *over*, but we find ways to get *through*.

I am not sure *exactly* why I felt the way I felt when I first discovered that another family had fallen apart. Perhaps it is that as a children's doctor, I see how families suffer when parents' relationships become frozen.

Another mental frozen state is when we allow our emotions to afflict us. I was the victim of this form of suffering until I discovered the RAIN method initially taught by Michele Macdonald and popularized by Tara Brach.

When we use the RAIN method to deal skillfully with emotions we Recognize them for what they are; we Allow them to be and we merely notice them without getting intimidated by them; we Investigate the root of these emotions and stay curious; and finally, we Never take our feelings too personally.

Despite the negative association we have when we think about being stuck and freezing alone, our pain and suffering can become our best teacher. We learn to surrender to what is. We can always choose to make the best of what we still have. The tide somehow finds a way to eventually come back. Conditions arise, but they also pass. We learn what it means to be at ease and in peace with the comings and goings of our troubles.

So, for those who are learning how a season of suffering through frozen relationships can be a challenge and specifically for those whose marriages are now going through a sad season, allow me to share the valuable life lesson running in the cold taught me:

- **There are indeed seasons to our lives. No season lasts forever.**

ALWAYS HAVE SOMETHING TO LOOK FORWARD TO

It was a muggy and humid day in Toronto. Apparently, it was a day where *even* the people who live there found the humidity far too high.

I live in a dry and dusty part of Canada, and needless to say, today I was dragging my behind to the finish line in one of the most unfavorable and bad luck circumstances one can ask for in long distance running. If anyone wants to run a painfully slow marathon, then pray for heat and humidity with no wind.

I had prayed for a fast marathon because I poured my heart fully into getting ready for the run in Toronto, a place at sea level rather than altitude. When one trains where I live, at 3,500 feet, running at sea level becomes an extra plus.

I heard God laugh…because there is a deep question with a funny answer that goes like this: "How do you make God laugh? You tell Him your plans."

My plan was to run a fast race and the humidity was beyond my control. Apparently, God had other plans for that particular day. My best and most sincere prayers went unanswered.

I also suddenly remembered the old Mother Goose rhyme which says:

For every ailment under the sun,

There is a remedy, or there is none;
If there be one, try to find it;
If there be none, never mind it.

It simply was so and could not be different. I trained hard, but the weather foiled my hard work. Nature sabotaged my plans and scuttled them to the bottom of the ocean. There was no point in sawing sawdust. I was done. Eventually, after much suffering, the run was thankfully almost over. *Only a few more miles and then the finish line*, I thought to myself.

I was keen to get this over with, once and for all. This messy marathon, on a rather fateful day, was one of the few I will not want to relive again. The humidity got worse and worse. It was almost suffocating.

Just as we passed what was then known as the Air Canada Center—home of the NBA World Champions of 2019—I ran at the same pace as another runner who glanced at my soaking wet body and asked me, "Where are you from?" When he heard I was from Alberta, he let out a profanity I cannot repeat here. He also added, "Man I am dying here, and I d*o not have a clue* how you are still running."

> When he heard I was from Alberta he let out a profanity I cannot repeat here. He also added, "Man I am dying here, and I do not have a clue how you are still running."

I have heard all kinds of coaches and spiritual teachers teach that it is important to be fully present at all times. They encourage one to say things like "Running…know that you are running" or "Be fully present right now." "You need not look toward the future, because that way you will miss out on the now", and they add, "You already have what you need— just pick up on it; patience in this moment will settle all future problems of your life."

Well, to be honest, these valuable insights may be generally true, but at that moment in muggy Toronto I wanted things to be *very, very* different!

After I crossed the finish line where I did not bother to look up at the cameras as they were capturing my fatigued body, I had something very different and pleasant to look forward to. The next day I was due to be at the local Mercedes dealership to take possession of a brand-new car.

Once I was back home, I quickly became aware of the dryness of the Prairies in an unstable, up-and-down-change-on-a-dime ecosystem, right next to the Rockies. Here wind gusts sweep over the Prairies often without pause and dry the air out in no time.

Incidentally, I read Ecclesiastes that day—chapter three to be exact—where it says, "For everything there is a season."

It was actually nice and warm in my hometown that day and as I flipped on the air conditioner of my new car, I remembered this:

- **There is a time to be in the now, but there is also a time to savour what lies ahead.**

PRE-RACE JITTERS

I once met a middle-aged lady who told me she trains for marathons but has never run one.

Hearing her story took me back to when I first heard a coach remind his clients that process matters more than outcome—that *what* we become in the process of preparing, matters more than the *actual* day of running a marathon.

Naturally, I asked her, "Why do you train so hard and so consistently and then get to a point where you are fit enough and strong enough to complete 26.2 miles, only to not do the run you clearly trained for?"

She responded by saying, "I always get so nervous around the time of actually having to run the marathon…and then I develop diarrhea. Since it is so sudden and intense, it impossible for me to find a washroom in time. I have tried everything, but nothing seems to work."

Her answer reminded me of a tool I use often. It is called permeation therapy.

One of the reasons that I am enthusiastic about cultivating mindfulness meditation, is that a deep inner state of quietness allows peace to permeate throughout my body. Many athletes get nervous at times—especially before the start of a marathon where anything can happen on any day. By allowing peaceful thoughts to pass unhindered through my mind and by remembering to stay skillful at training and taming the mind I have been able to avoid pre-race jitters close to 99% of the time.

The Chinese call the gut the second brain. Scientists tell us there is a gut-brain axis. When the lady runner told me about her diarrhea around the time of marathons I was not surprised.

I wish I knew about the benefits of mindful meditation when I met her. I could have shared some of my experiences and encouraged her to use the benefits of mindfulness meditation to keep her calm and peaceful. Earlier I mentioned the WWFU concept—whatever works for you. Mindfulness does not work for everyone, but it works for many.

As I wrote in a previous chapter, Yogi Berra, the famous baseball player, observed that: "Baseball is 90% mental. The other half is physical." Marathon running and the successful conquering of fears are possible, but first we must prepare the mind—process always precedes outcome.

- **See the jitters of life as hidden opportunities which teach us to become stronger.**

FEAR FACTOR

There used to be a show on TV called Fear Factor. It was very popular until it met the fate of most TV shows. People get bored by the same patterns and switch channels to another seemingly new-never-seen-before show. Newness attracts but staleness is inevitable as Larry King and Oprah's lifespans on TV teach us.

In the show contestants had to face heights, deal with various extreme uncertainties and consume all kinds of dubious food and drinks. These fears were mostly triggered by physical factors. But how about fears rooted in non-physical causes?

Marathon running taught me a few things about fear.

> Fear is the second strongest force out there.

It has been said that fear is the second strongest force out there; that only faith is stronger. Faith means so much more than a religious term to me. It also means a deep and unwavering *trust* in a realistic, positive belief system. The kind of faith that appeals to many is reflected by the fact that the famous book by Dr. Peale was originally called "The Power of Faith" until the publishers changed it to "The Power of Positive Thinking."

Fear harbored in a mind is fear that can keep us away from a finish line we would have crossed had we made different choices. Someone once observed that fear tolerated is faith contaminated. It is so very, very true.

Fear is what holds many back in life. We fear the unknown. We wonder if we ever will be able to reach goals we set and then we "readjust" and end up aiming lower. Compromised living becomes justified. We mediate on imaginations of what can go wrong. We use our logical brain—the left brain—to convince ourselves of whatever narratives serves us the best. We justify whatever fears we choose and make excuses for why fear is on the podium. These unskillful mental formations often cause us to suffer more than we have to. In short, many of us get comfortable functioning in our *dys*function.

The antidote to fear is not courage…but love.

- **When facing fears, seek the presence of love, and know perfect love never fails to get rid of fear.**

VOICE OF FEAR

I have a good friend who is also a doctor and a runner. Sadly, his marriage fell apart. As a result, he is suffering deeply and daily. He is on a dark inner journey of discovering ways to manage suffering more skillfully.

During one of our morning runs he was feeling particularly down. All I could do was to share with him what one of my teachers shared with me, which is: In this life there are only two voices—the voice of fear or the voice of love. Elsewhere in this book I have often referred to the voice of fear versus the voice of love. It really is this simple once we distill all there is to consider regarding our emotions and how we choose to respond to them.

A few days after that particular run he texted me and shared that this insight helped him greatly. It gave him a new perspective. As we all know, the color of our lenses tends to color the world we look at. How we look at things determine how those things look. Few things matter as much as cultivating wise perception.

Many times, when I am out there in the heat, the cold, the sleet, the ice, but also in the pristine weather of Hawaii or San Diego, I am reminded that we all can choose what frequency to dial in to. Animals cannot do what we do—they are incapable and unaware. They do not have our option of choosing an attitude.

The Bible has one verse which says it so well—for me at least. It says that we must cast down all *imaginations* and bring every *thought* captive to the obedience of Truth.

One year during the Boston Marathon I encountered what is known as Heart Break Hill. Legend has it that a local hero, Johnny Kelly was in the lead during this iconic race. He was overtaken at this hill by another runner. As this runner passed him, he gently patted Johnny on his butt as if to say, "Too bad and too sad, but this is where I take over and beat you to the finish line."

I did not find Heartbreak Hill as hard as other runners had me believe prior to the Boston Marathon, but there were many other races in the hundred plus marathons I completed where I learned that there were times when it was my determination that kept me running. My body had told me to throw in the towel long ago. It was a case of mind over matter.

That is why I sometimes do something odd: I read my own book, the one I wrote a few years ago (*Moving Forward*).

In the end we get to ignore the voice of fear. That is the voice that tells us we are no good; we do not have what it takes; we are a fraud; we are not as good as our "buddy" over there; we will not finish; if only people know what we think when we are alone; we could have been better at whatever; we will be addicted forever; we can never be married again; and on and on it goes inside our heads. Almost like a long tennis rally, the shots go back and forth in our heads.

I recently read a quote attributed to President Calvin Coolidge, the thirtieth president of the United States:

> "Nothing in the world can take the place of persistence. Talent will not; nothing is more common than unsuccessful men with talent. Genius will not; unrewarded genius is almost a proverb. Education will not: the world is full of educated derelicts. Persistence and determination alone are omnipotent."

Persistence indeed is the ability to overcome life's inevitable troubles by consistently listening to the powerful voice of love. Once again as I wrote elsewhere, in Hawaii there is a word in their language which describes the idea of being resilient and always finding ways to persist in the quest to move forward. The word is Imua. I have tattooed this word indelibly on my subconscious mind.

Marathon running, more than anything else in life, taught me this key lesson:

- **Listen to the voice of love and ignore the voice of fear by switching to a channel that serves you better.**

STRUGGLE A LITTLE LESS

I was reading recently in Canada's National Newspaper, *The Globe and Mail*, about something we tend to take for granted: tea.

Apparently in 1952, on October 3 to be exact, the British could finally drink as much tea as they wanted. Prior to that time tea was rationed. In 1940, as a legacy of WWII, the government decided to limit the amount of tea one could drink. Fortunately for tea-lovers, in 1952 that limit was lifted.

What on earth does this story have to do with running marathons or for that matter life itself you say? Or for that matter about the functioning of the mind?

Everything I say. Everything about how the way we train our mind impacts the way we suffer.

> Life is imperfect, impermanent and we should not take things so personally.

When we struggle, we often forget ancient truths taught long ago, but still true today: life is imperfect, impermanent, and we should not take things so personally. Unless we accept these truths, we will suffer. As long as we sense we are struggling we will lack equanimity.

I have learned the hard way that struggles—not just attempts to cover more than 100 marathons—always have an expiration date. Nothing lasts for ever. Pain arises and then goes. Sometimes it takes a bit longer. By staying patient and acknowledging we all have a kinship of struggling together to get to our finish lines, we actually keep on moving forward and in the right direction. We are not stuck. We head in the right direction and we do it in a customized manner.

We may end up facing all kinds of people and events in our lives we did not want or did not choose, but it is what we got anyway. Dung gets delivered. Life is unfair. Stuff happens. Some of us win the lottery in reverse. Feelings and experiences of extreme unsatisfactoriness are common and not unusual. It's a mistake to briefly think we are the only ones who experience that.

So meanwhile…don't struggle so hard; enjoy every step along the way and know that we live in a world of abundance and if we are meant to get our proverbial tea back…we will. And if it is not our destiny to get what we want then we might as well blow against the wind or compete with thunder when we let out an explosive and foul amount of gas from our rectums.

- **Every test we are given has a beginning and an end. The low tide always makes way for the high tide.**

MISSING THE MARK

They say there is much power in telling a story. Apparently, stories stir us emotionally. Facts tell and stories sell. When that happens an idea sticks.

To illustrate let's remind ourselves of something that happened slightly over 2,000 years ago.

Jesus was trying to teach his followers to be compassionate to all. He used a story of the Jewish man who was attacked and left half dead beside the road. In the story, religious people passed this man by and pretended they did not see his needs. In those days, people from Samaria, a region in the Middle East, were despised and not respected at all. A Good Samaritan stopped when he saw the Jewish man in need and helped him out by soothing his wounds and paying for his convalescence in a nearby inn.

It is indeed a story of being *truly* helpful. It is a story of lovingkindness and compassion. A story where color of skin or place of origin played no role. But it is also a story of missing an opportunity to match one's beliefs with one's actions. The religious types ignored the man who needed kindness.

But before we judge them, let's look at our own shortcomings. We all are guilty of missing the mark when it comes to being truly helpful.

Missing the mark sometimes can end up with a positive outcome.

There is a more recent story of Massimo Bottura, a famous chef who runs one of the world's most popular restaurants in Modena, Italy. His restaurant, Osteria Francescana is rated very highly by Michelin. To get a table is hard—one has to book months in advance.

Yet this restaurant almost did not make it in the beginning. Massimo was ready to quit. He had enough. His American wife and sacred soul mate encouraged him to give it *just one more year* before throwing in the towel. He listened to her wise words: "If you give up now you will regret it for the rest of your life."

Like all of us Massimo made some mistakes along the way. But he never gave up. One day one of his chefs dropped a very delicate dish—a lemon tart. The poor fellow was sure Massimo would fire him on the spot.

> And so it is in life. Receive a broken lemon tart with joy and taste it for what it is.

But that did not happen. Today if you were to visit his fine restaurant in Modena, Italy, you will find on the menu a dish named "Oops! I dropped the Lemon Tart." The restaurant actually serves a broken-up lemon tart. It is delicious. And it is available because of what some call a reframe—when we look at something that went wrong, supposedly, and turn it into a plus. It is where we take a minus and change it into a plus by drawing a vertical line. And so it is in life. Receive a broken lemon tart with joy and taste it for what it is.

What can we do when we miss the mark? We can simply try again. We can remind ourselves that we are not in peace because we may have chosen an action that did not match who we really are. We can show compassion toward ourselves and ask for mercy. We can remain gentle with ourselves.

Then we move forward and, like a marathon runner, continue to press toward the mark, expending all the energy that we have left, or we find new ways to create the energy we may need.

I have noticed over the years that, generally speaking, people who press toward the mark with the most confidence and peace—people who are aware of their spiritual dimensions—live by the ideals expressed in The Healers Prayer from *A Course in Miracles:*

I am here only to be truly helpful. I am here to represent Him who sent me.
I do not have to worry about what to say or what to
do, because He who sent me will direct me.
I am content to be wherever He wishes, knowing He goes there with me.
I will be healed as I let Him teach me to heal.

When we are certain of our goal and purpose we press on and find new ways to be truly helpful to others and ourselves. Marathon running taught me that even when we miss the mark we try again at a later moment.

- **Every experienced marathon runner at some point misses a mark and either drops out or runs slower than expected. The great ones *always* come back and try again.**

NEW TERRITORY

The one and only ultra-marathon I ever did took place at the Southern tip of Africa. In an earlier chapter I gave you one lesson learned then. Here is another one from the same pivotal moment during the quest to push myself as far as I could go and, in the process, make some discoveries about myself.

Prior to the year 2000 there was a lot of fear—fear that as soon as the planet changed from 1999 to 2000 the world would go into a tailspin; technology would fail; doom and gloom was on the horizon.

Fear is a currency used regularly and without fail during every political election season. Fear will always be with us. Like a dark shadow it follows us wherever we are anywhere between the two poles of this planet.

Fear in 2000 was also a factor in creating huge incomes for people who cashed in on others' beliefs that the world may come to an end. These "experts" were paid lots of money to build in systems to "beat" the so-called Y2K collapse of all things technological.

As I lined up with mostly South African runners in the cool, dark predawn ocean air of Cape Town, I had no idea what would happen when I entered a new territory. I trained hard for my first extra-long distance of 56 kilometers. I never ran further than 42.2 kilometers in a race.

One of the most memorable moments took place at the 42.2 kilometer mark. Unlike all of my other marathons there was no finish line—14 more kilometers were still waiting to be conquered.

At the time I was fully present and in the moment. The flow-state was amazing. I felt like Forrest Gump in that I could go on and on and on. As I entered this new territory, I was surprised to be in the zone mentally. However, a few miles later I experienced a sudden shift as the accumulation of lactic acid in my muscles slowed me down.

A few minutes earlier I was sure the end would come too soon. Now I wondered if I would ever reach the end! I had to remind myself that I did the training for this event. All I had to do was slow down and wait for a second breath to arrive. And it did eventually arrive as expected. That is what happens when we decide to endure.

Many years later, looking back I realized this important lesson:

- **When your life takes you in unchartered territory, relax and trust your training. Fear may want to remind you of the facts. Ignore it.**

MA'ALAHI

Looking down from 35,000 feet at the snow-covered mountains from my window seat, I was savoring a cup of fine Italian coffee. I believe that coffee is full of antioxidants and polyphenols. Yes, it can cause harm if one drinks too much, but my own research convinced me there are some health benefits.

On the side of the coffee paper cup, these words caught my eye: *Savour the journey. One step at a time.*

The airline obviously employed skilled marketing gurus—perhaps from Madison Avenue in New York. The words were simple, but very, very inspiring.

They also reminded me of the most common answer I give when people ask me why I have chosen to run every day of my life as long as I have a heart that beats, breath that fills my lungs, and legs that move me along at whatever pace I decide upon.

It is simply this: whatever you do, make sure you savour every moment and do it one step at a time. Step by step by step. Moment by moment by moment. In Hawaii they refer to keeping things simple as Ma'alahi (pronounced as Mah-ah-lah-hee).

After being told by my fitness tracker how many steps a recent marathon involved, I was curious how many steps 100 marathons added up to.

My calculator told me it was 5.25 million! And every step counted. It was that simple.

I also calculated how far I ran over the past 26 years and it boils down to 78,579 kilometers or:

—Seventeen times between New York City and Los Angeles.

—Fourteen times between New York City and London, England.

—Five-and a half times around Australia.

Out of all those steps, I then wondered which one was the most important.

If I buy into the teaching of the Tao, the answer is obvious: the first step counts the most because a journey of a thousand steps begins with the first step. No first step; no journey. It is that simple. Ma'alahi.

I am counting all the steps, amazed that I am "renting" a body which enabled me thus far to take 5.25 million steps and more.

During the majority of my marathons, at some point I was ready to give up, but I decided to endure to the very end. One step at a time. Moment by moment to the very end, savoring the journey; knowing that pain always passes. What never passes is the joy of overcoming.

We all suffer at some point and time due to the fact that life tends to give us what we do not want: an unexpected loss of a dear one, an unwelcome diagnosis by a doctor, a call from a lawyer informing us of some bad news coming our way, a bank balance that invites a declaring of bankruptcy, a spouse who calmly informs us that although relationships are for a reason, a season or a lifetime, this one is not for a lifetime. Now it's over. Finished forever.

I have observed as a doctor, dealing with a wide variety of issues — both physical and mental—that the patients who do the best during the inevitable vicissitudes of living, are the ones who take one step at a time, wisely knowing the difference between focusing on what they can control and letting go of that which is out of their control.

These are simple truths and yet they are not easy to apply day-by-day.

- **Step by step we arrive at goals that matter to us. Savor the journey, one step at a time.**

BE AMAZED

As an endurance athlete, I am very aware of the critical role our breath plays as we propel ourselves forward mile after mile after mile.

I am always amazed and grateful when I remember the big role my breath plays in being mindful, but also in keeping me going –even when I am fast asleep and unaware of my own breathing.

Because my writing and running are virtually intertwined I tend to keep interesting articles for later use. One such an article was written almost twenty years ago in Canada's national Newspaper, The Globe and Mail.

Allan Fotheringham reminded his readers of numerous reasons to be grateful.

Allan explained that if you could shrink the earth's population to a village of precisely 100 people, with all existing human ratios remaining the same, then 70 would be non-white and 30 white. Six people would possess 60% of the entire world's wealth. A great number (80%) would live in substandard housing. Seventy out of a 100 people would not be able to read, and only one would have a university education. The vast majority would not own a computer. Just having food in the fridge and a roof over your head would make you richer than 75% of the world's population. If you had spare change in a dish somewhere you would be among only 8% of this planet.

---

* For more information on what it would look like if the world's population were 100 people, see www.ed.ted.com/best_of_web/5rhHgDwh

Most of us when facing setbacks and obstacles focus on what we lack when in truth we still have a lot to be thankful for. It is so easy to take things for granted and to feel like a victim at times.

I read about a man who felt sorry for himself; his business went down the drain slowly, and it impacted his health. He had to make a trip to the bank to work with financial experts there. He needed a new plan. He was in dire straits.

He felt deeply sorry for himself…

Then suddenly he saw coming toward him a man with no legs. The man was sitting on a wooden platform equipped with wheels from roller skates. He moved forward by using blocks of wood in each hand. As the two men passed, the man with no legs beamed a warm smile to our friend who felt very down in the dumps—until he encountered the handicapped brother, smiling warmly and wishing all a happy day as he passed them on his wooden platform.

It reminds all of us of a saying I keep close by to remind myself to always be grateful for what I have. I wish I knew the author who said this:

> *I had the blues because I had no shoes,*
> *Until upon the street, I met a man who had no feet.*

Not every human being thinks of the breath in terms of exercise, but a fellow traveler and podcast host, Adam Markel, whom I frequently listen to during the many miles of marathon training, always reminds the listeners of a universal truth all of us so easily forget:

- **Every morning when you wake up, take a deep breath, and know that as you breathe in, somewhere on the planet, another person is taking in a final breath.**

THE BIGGEST NEED

In 1954 a man with an amazing brain left us with a lasting legacy. He pondered the most basic human needs and ended up with the *five* common needs we all have.

Today, mental health experts and behavioral scientists refer to Maslow's Hierarchy of Needs as one of the best, if not the definitive, models to try and understand and explain why we behave the way we do. Maslow took his time to ponder human needs and developed his model between 1943 and 1954. It was first published in *Motivation and Personality*.

Maslow's Hierarchy of Needs are:

—physiological needs

—safety needs

—love and belonging needs (to feel connected to one's tribe)

—esteem needs (to feel worthy and noticed)

—self-actualization needs

Discussing how meeting these needs impacts our behavior will take up enough space to fill a library.

People have asked me why I decided to run as much as I did and continue to do at a less intense level.

> It is not about running per se as it is about…
> how running is a metaphor.

I find it easy to answer and usually say it is not about the running per se as much as it is about how such a habit reveals to me who I am, and how running is a metaphor for so many chapters in all our lives. My motive is all about a way of investigating personal development, not just for my sake but also the sake of others I am honored to help.

Scriptures teach that athletes press toward a mark of a higher calling; that we run the race set before us with endurance; that we run for a crown that perishes; that we refuse to allow the weight of worry that so easily slows us down to hold us back; and that we are more than conquerors through God who gives us strength.

Life coaches remind us that we are to run in our own lane—mind your own attitude and refuse to judge others, control others, fix others and instead focus with a laser-sharp intensity on the only thing you really get to control: our own behaviors. Ultimately, we do not control the behavior of others.

When we pay attention to people who are hospice workers and who earned the right to comment on what most humans say on their deathbed, because they have been there and thus able to spot consistent patterns, we always here this:

The only thing that truly matters is how we loved others and how we were loved.

As much as I can say like the actor in *Chariots of Fire*, one of my favorite movies, "God made me for a purpose and when I run, I feel God's pleasure", I am always reminded that in the end our biggest need is indeed to know we are loved and to make the most of every opportunity to unconditionally and with great kindness and compassion love all creatures.

It is not easy. Some may even say it is impossible. I agree totally that it is impossible.

But, as the Buddha taught thousands of years ago, we live in a world that is imperfect and if we think that simply doing everything right will end these imperfections, we are delusional and we will suffer for sure.

The point is to alleviate suffering and to *aspire* to reduce imperfections, knowing we will never reach perfection. When we cultivate this aspiration frequently, we end up bringing hope, light, and healing to those we encounter, so often not by accident but on purpose.

If I were perfect, then during every daily run, I would be thinking more about others and *their* needs rather than my own needs. But I aspire to use my runs as meditation time also and in doing so I remember this:

- **The biggest need is to feel loved and to make sure we let others know we love them.**

OUTWORN

Since 1992 I have run an average of 3,000 kilometres every year.

The same brand of running shoes carried me over those distances, but each and every pair, came to a place in time when it needed to be replaced.

What in your life needs to be replaced? What no longer serves you?

I have observed over the forty years of working as a doctor, that three key areas dominate when it comes to our vitality: our health, our finances and our relationships. I even asked pastor friends of mine to name the top three prayer requests of the people they shepherd. It always seems to be centered on health, finances and relationships.

Maybe you are no longer being served by making poor choices in terms of the food you regularly consume. Maybe it is time to throw away ideas that have served you and look at new ways to improve the way you eat.

Maybe some object you cling to no longer serves you and you know that it is outworn and cannot help you any longer. The time may come to let it go.

Or maybe in the financial realm you have a career which no longer meets your needs, and it is time to say you and the career must part; it has served its purpose; now is the time to pivot into a new direction and create better ways to reach your financial goals.

I sat in my study a while ago and simply looked at the wall next to my desk for longer than usual.

I am blessed to have trained in Houston at the Texas Children's hospital where I learned how to care for children and youth trying to lose weight, eat healthy foods and exercise appropriately.

When I returned to Canada, I launched a pediatric obesity clinic which caught the attention of Canada's national newspaper, The Globe and Mail. This paper ran two very complimentary pieces about our clinic, and I chose to laminate them and put them on the wall of my study.

This was the wall which one day captured my undivided attention.

After just sitting there, certain that my run cleared my mind like the windshield of a car which needed to be cleaned to get better vision, I now felt I could see clearly.

As a result of my usual reflective state and a protracted time of pondering deeply, I got up slowly and removed the articles I framed and hung on the wall.

Why did I do that with a deep sense of certainty that it was the *absolute* right thing to do?

They no longer served me. This clinic came and went. It was there for a reason and a season. Its destiny was not to last any longer. Once our local pediatric hospital discovered the importance of caring for obese children, they used government support and launched their own clinic. I applied to be part of their team and got rejected.

In Canada, most Canadians believe that health care should be free. Many Canadians, because of their high taxes, consider health care a fundamental right. People are not prepared to pay for a service if they can get their government to pay for it with a taxpayer-funded model. This attitude resulted in a slow death of our clinic.

This clinic which brought me so much joy and purpose was not meant to continue. That particular clinic started for a reason, but only lasted a season.

What is hanging on the wall in the place of the articles which praised the weight clinic for children and youth when I launched it a few years ago is something *completely* different.

Before I typed these words, I looked briefly at the same wall and read:

> "Share your knowledge. It is a way
> to achieve immortality." (Words spoken by the Dalai Lama)

These words continue to meet me when I write or do any work in the study. They are there for a reason, a season and a lifetime. I will always keep them close by to remind me why I share my knowledge on TV and radio, in the newspaper, and in the exam rooms where I encounter patients.

They serve me well just like all the dozens and dozens of Nike running shoes over the past few decades of running marathons. But the shoes are different: once it is over it is over. The time comes to move on and to let the past go. It is never as easy to do as it may sound. It is said in Buddhism that one of the most important questions to ask is "What is expected of me in this situation?"

I know the answer when it comes to letting go of the past and the answer is simple:

- **Do not cling to that which no longer serves you.**

THE OBNOXIOUS SHIRT

In my closet are a number of T shirts. Along some past marathon routes are also a number of my T shirts. What happened?

Some were tossed and some were kept. The ones with obnoxious colors were the ones I used at the start of a run when fall marathons can be cold until the sun rises. When it became too hot, I tossed such a shirt along the route somewhere, knowing that the course would get swept later and clothing would be given to the poor and needy.

If one is crazy enough to run as much as I do, then after a few hundred races there are simply too many shirts. My wife by the way can tell you so much more about my closet with too many shirts. I know the day is coming where some major culling will just *have* to take place.

But one shirt that was indeed "obnoxious" with its bright yellow color screaming at me from far away is one I kept. It was a Boston Marathon shirt. As a very average runner I have only made it to Boston twice. So, I kept it and wear it only indoors, mostly concerned that the bright yellow color would blind others outside.

Not so long ago the organizers of a local marathon which I have participated in almost every year since 1992 wanted all the shirts over the past 50 years for a 50th anniversary display. They were missing a few and contacted me to see if I had the particular years' shirts. Luckily, I did.

When it comes to over 100 finishers medals it is a different story. I have kept all the medals handed to me at the finish line from race number three to the most recent one. These medals tend to take up less space.

But what happened to race one and two?

Those marathons took place in Africa and at the time marathons were not far enough to justify a medal—only ultra-marathons mattered and even to this day when I visit South Africa it seems there will always be a few runners who don't even count marathons. Only ultra-marathons matter.

Who knows what will happen when my wife and I declutter our home one day in a season of downsizing? In preparation I am already more selective with holding on to obnoxious shirts that shout. As I learn more about life and the fact that nothing lasts forever, I am on a steep learning curve to travel more lightly.

My wide repertoire of marathon running shirts taught me this:

- **Travel lightly. Let go of that which may bring back good memories, but no longer has a purpose in your life.**

KINDNESS TOWARD SELF

One of my rituals is to learn on the run. I refer to it as "grow on the go." A great podcast I listened to twice during a recent run went deeper into what it means to be kind to oneself.

At the time of writing this book, we have a leader in the USA— a leader most see as a man with a titanic ego. His name triggers a wide variety of emotions in the minds of millions. He is known for his self-absorption. But self-compassion is vastly different from self-absorption.

One thing is crystal clear to me: It is easy to confuse ego with self-care.

Self-care is known by other names: wellness; pacing wisely; self-respect; unselfish selfishness (supposedly by focusing on self in a healthy manner we have more to give to others…unselfishly); self-compassion; and many other versions which all say this:

—-*Remember to be your own best friend*

When Christ was asked to summarize all of Scriptures referred to by some as The Law, He answered, "Love God, and love your neighbor as yourself." That is rather specific and succinct.

The sad part about this important sentence is that many religious and spiritual teachers focus only on two things that were said: love God and love others. The self-part is conveniently ignored.

I suspect they ignore the third part (love yourself) because they are worried that by teaching self-compassion, they will create selfish souls.

In the Zen tradition we are reminded that, just like a bird or a plane needs two wings to fly, we too need to have two wings to soar—compassion and wisdom.

These two qualities must be in balance always.

When we show compassion to ourselves it also helps others. When we feel our own worthiness, we are better able to help others feel theirs. People at peace are less likely to harm others in word or deed—let alone harm themselves.

- **Do not allow yourself to feed off the scraps falling from the table. You are worthy to take a seat at the table.**

WORKS IN PROGRESS

About ten percent into a 26.2 mile run I started a conversation with a fellow from California. I guessed that he may have been ten years older than me. After only a few minutes we felt a connection; a joining; a commonality. Our momentum forward was effortless—in unison; like a metronome maintaining a regular back-and-forth. As I read what I wrote here, I still remember hearing our feet land softly, but swiftly on the streets of San Francisco.

I really enjoy marathons where there is no rush—no need to stay focused every second and monitor one's heart rate, pace and state of mind. It is fun to simply be in the moment and connect with other runners. After all, we all are in this together. Runners become a brotherhood or sisterhood—anywhere and anytime where marathons are held.

After a few minutes, I learned that my new friend was a grandfather; that his family will meet him at the half-way mark; that this was his 12th marathon; and that he runs because he loves to eat. Running —at least that was his version of things—was one of the best ways to burn off calories. As you will read in a chapter in this book on what I learned on a cruise ship, you will see that my friend was wrong. However, I did not want to rain on his parade.

At one point there was a long moment of quietness. The only sound was our breathing, our strides hitting the asphalt, the waves of the Pacific Ocean rhythmically rolling to shore and the occasional shout of seagulls hovering above us. I also heard two ladies behind us in deep conversation.

My new friend asked me, "So...how many marathons have you done?" I answered, "This is my 110ᵗʰ marathon."

> There was no need to say much because we knew that we all are works in progress; each one with a unique story.

Suddenly one of the ladies behind us shouted "Holy F##K!!!"

I did not realize these ladies heard our conversation. I could not help it. I just had to burst out laughing at her response and looked back. We invited them to join us. Now we had four people running in our pack, discussing life as marathon runners. We bonded. There was no need to say much because we knew that we all are works in progress; each one with a unique story.

So it is with life. We may not all be running together, but we all are works in progress, on a quest to somewhere, different from one another, experiencing our unique conscious pivots along the path. But like waves, we all belong to the same ocean.

When people hear about my quest, they make comments such as, "I have never done a marathon. I only run five K's." (Five Kilometers)

I usually ask them to recalibrate their thinking and drop the word "only". I am told one of my strengths is to encourage others, so I tell them, "You are figuring out what works for you. Listen to your own heart. Do not compete or compare. Life is not a race, but it is a long journey. Be who you are and enjoy figuring out your own progress. Be real. Be you. Be the *best* you wherever you may be on this journey."

Give yourself permission to be a work in progress. On the path to love (as Rumi said), friends and strangers are one and the same.

We may not *always* remember it, but we are loved, and we have the potential to love others better.

How about starting with the easy part which is by bonding with those who match our energy. They are way easier to love than our enemies. And both Jesus and the Buddha said the same thing about love and goodwill toward all. I will paraphrase it the way I remember these wise words:

> *—love all your enemies and forgive them, for your*
> *own sake, more than any other reason.*

Another thing Jesus taught, which resonates so much with me: *As much as you did it to the least of these you did it to me.*

The Dalai Lama, I believe, may have said once, "Be kind for selfish reasons." Now that is a mouthful and most of us may take a bit of time to digest the deep truth in those wise words.

The day after another San Francisco Marathon I found myself next to the Pacific Ocean. It was a usual foggy day. Those days are the days the Bay Area so often encounters in "Summer."

Two things stood out for me as I paused in a cool mist while staring over the Pacific Ocean, the wind gently touching my grateful face and my mind filled with zero fog. It may have been foggy that day but in my mind, I experienced 20/20 visual clarity that we all are works in progress.

I had a *deep* inner knowing that improvement starts with me, and that I am to…

- **Stay very patient with myself and be comfortable with the real me. We all are works in progress.**

DEFAULT

Over the past 30 years of running, I have seen so many spectacular advancements from basic tools to monitor fitness, to today's technology which, at times, requires a PhD to master fully.

One thing never changed: default settings.

Currently my fitness tracker has the pace as its default setting. Some athletes use devices to track their daily steps, distance, or how many floors they climb in 24 hours.

I suppose there are ways to change default settings to suit one's own style or preferences. Somehow all the devices I have used over the years left their factories with a determination to always start off with a specific default setting.

This got me thinking: We monitor our fitness with trackers, but how do we monitor our default mindset settings?

> All of us throughout the day, get to choose our perceptions, words, thoughts, attitudes and actions.

All of us throughout the day get to choose our perceptions, words, thoughts, attitudes and actions. Some of us have positive default settings such as optimism, quickness to forgive, cultivating calmness at all times, looking for ways to have a perception which always frames situations in a positive light.

I have found a daily meditation practice often linked to my daily run helps me cultivate ideal default settings. Of course, this practice done early in the day becomes the foundation for the rest of that day. It sets the tone. It determines the trajectory.

I remember reading that the Dalai Lama once was asked "Do you ever get angry?" His immediate answer was priceless, and not what the questioner anticipated.

"Of course, I get angry…but I do not stay angry for long," this influential spiritual teacher answered.

- **Good habits are cultivated over time. But unless we cultivate them daily, our default settings tend to take over.**

MOZART IN THE MORNING

In my time zone, around ten in the morning, on most days, I try not to run.

Instead, I try to be close to my desktop computer. So far, this customized plan has served me very well and here is why.

At that time, ideally, I want to have internet access. I am too cheap to use my smartphone to connect because it "chews up" lots of data, and where I live data costs are extraordinarily high—more than in most other countries on this planet, most likely because the majority of Canadians are too meek and mild to demand lower rates. I once read that when the question was asked, "How does one get 100 Canadians to get out of a pool?" the answer was to simply tell them, "Get out of the pool."

Because of the high roaming charges, I am usually by a computer, connected to the Worldwide Web at ten in the mornings and the least of my worries is to limit airtime at that point.

Let me explain that I am a devoted fan of both Mozart and San Francisco. My favorite classical music station, based in San Francisco, often called the City by the Bay has a daily segment called "Mozart in the Morning." I rarely miss my moments with Mozart.

Of course one can download his music and take it anywhere, but the nostalgic part of me prefers to hear it broadcast, live, from San Francisco.

By the way. I think another reason I enjoy listing to the station is that it gives me updates: good and bad ones.

The good news? "It is another beautiful day in the Bay area with plenty of sunshine today and for the next few days." As I listen to these words, working on this book, I am watching snowflakes by my window and noticing the naked trees in our backyard, knowing the leaves will come back…but *only* eight months from now and then these leaves will only last for three to four months at the most.

The bad news? "There are a few accidents to report; one on the Bay Bridge and the other on the Golden Gate Bridge. Traffic is very heavy today. Allow yourself lots of extra time to get to work." Meanwhile where I live traffic is a mess, but it's a small M mess. I can get to work without a calendar. Time is indeed "wasted" sitting in traffic jams…but not as much as in other bigger cities.

And besides…in my car, satellite radio gives me the option of more Mozart and after an invigorating morning run, it is truly a privilege to sit back and enjoy another form of meditation.

- **It has been said that love makes the world go round, but may I add that in addition to love, the global appeal of great music comes in a close second.**

NOURISH

I read recently, using my cell phone to catch up on the morning news, that Volkswagen has its own brand of sausage in Germany and they sell more sausages than cars! But are sausages the best way to nourish oneself?

A number of the world's top athletes, who also happen to be vegan, will never consume sausages made by Volkswagen. They elect to pay close attention to ways they nourish their bodies.

If triathletes, endurance freaks who endure not just marathons, but also swimming and cycling, have cultivated the art of balance, then it seems to me that balanced nourishment matters a lot if we are to endure. That is why I tend to think of life as a balance between our spiritual existence, our physical being and also our thinking process. Sort of like a three-legged stool.

We either nourish ourselves mindfully or mindlessly. We go deep, or we go superficial.

> NEST Method:
> -Nutrition
> -Exercise
> -Sleep
> -Thinking positive

If the three-legged metaphor fails, how about the metaphor of a vehicle's four wheels? To be well one has to balance nutrition, exercise, sleep, and our thinking minds. (I mentioned earlier that I refer to this as my own NEST method—Nutrition, Exercise, Sleep and Thoughts.)

On the same day I read about Volkswagen making sausages, I had to plug in my phone. Never before did I enjoy this activity of "nourishing" my phone with fresh power as much as I did on that particular day. Charging a phone being the highlight of the day? Not exactly, for most of us, but this is what led up to my own excitement.

My phone collected dirt and dust over the years, and it "blocked" a proper fit for the charging jack. While away from Canada to do a marathon in the US, I discovered that this finicky connection was going to derail my ability to use my phone while away from home.

As soon as I got back home I was "saved" by a friendly man—for no charge, he cleaned out the jack where one plugs in a charger cord and now all is well. The phone is easily nourished.

While running back from the very helpful repairman's clinic where my phone got healed, the thought occurred to me: how often do we allow dirt to come in the way of our nourishment and power?

In order to endure in life, we must protect our nourishment diligently and daily. It is easy to do it for a reason and a season. But how about a lifetime? How can we sustain healthy nourishment?

So far, my own spiritual nourishment is to stay plugged in to my Higher Power daily. As the saying goes, the main thing is to keep the main thing the main thing.

My mental nourishment is rooted in a daily habit of meditation early in the day using a method taught by Zen masters (Insight Meditation). I am convinced that the way we see things, our perception, determines what we think, and in turn what we feel, and in turn what we say or do.

We nourish our souls by resting before we get tired.

I have learned from the writings of Dale Carnegie that our hearts spend more time resting than working. Pro-active rest pays off huge dividends in our quest to endure. And as an athlete who trained for and completed over 100 marathons, I think my heart deserves to rest more than it works!

When we allow our hearts to rest and tune in to what really matters, we arrive at what they refer to in Hawaii as Na'au (Pronounced Nah-ow, meaning unification of the heart and mind).

Nourishing oneself with sausages or not and being properly plugged in, free from "dirt" blocking the flow of energy…these all are personal choices.

- **Figure out what your own, unique nourishment looks like. Then follow that path consistently.**

RITUALS

When I was training for my first Boston Marathon, I had a ritual of always checking the news before I set out for my pre-dawn early morning runs. I do not do that anymore. I shall explain why later.

In reading a newspaper prior to my run, I discovered that on October 2, 1950 only nine newspapers published a certain cartoon. This cartoon and an acorn seed share a common truth: all big things start small.

Later, around the 1960's, this cartoon ran in 2,600 newspapers in 75 countries. It had a peak readership of 355 million people at one point.

I am talking about Charles M. Schultz's cartoon strip, *Peanuts*.

Mr. Schultz drew almost 1800 *Peanuts* strips before he died in 2000. This was his consistent daily ritual.

Another creative man, Tom Woolfe, had this ritual: he dressed up in fancy clothes (he was known for his dapper brand), and secluded himself in his writing space daily. This ritual allowed him to be a prolific producer of books devoured by millions all over the globe.

> Mine happens to be one of having consistent priorities: every day after I rise and pee, I train my spiritual muscles, then my mental muscles and then my running muscles. Always in that order.

I cannot tell you which ritual to choose in your own life. Mine happens to be one of having consistent priorities: every day after I rise and pee, I train my spiritual muscles, then my mental muscles and then my running muscles. Always in that order. These are my core values.

By the way, this method is one I adopted from Davidji, a master meditation teacher who calls it his RPM method: rise, pee, meditate.

The return on investing time always seems to be certain and high. I intentionally *make* the time to be grateful, to focus on my breath, to utter positive affirmations, and to do some critical stretches which I learned from my caring yoga teachers. Over the years I see no reason to change this daily ritual. But that is just what works for me. We all have to customize what works for us.

Considering the return on investments is why I refuse to fill my mind with what newspapers have to dish up the beginning of each day. I'd rather learn from the Buddha or Jesus or other spiritual masters first and then later, if I have a few extra minutes, allow the newspapers to feed me with their version of truth. Sadly, their standards over the years have dropped to new lows of being blatant and unapologetically biased rather than reporting the news.

To be fair…the Peanuts story from the newspaper was a good story amidst all the political vitriol.

Zig Ziglar, the renowned motivational speaker used to say, "I read both the newspaper and the Bible every day…that way I know what both sides are up to."

I have found in my own life that my spiritual roots must come first. It is a bit like a tree: we can see the leaves, but what us unseen—the roots— determine the leaves.

- **I have observed that one of the key differences between successful and mediocre lives has to do with the quality of morning rituals.**

PHOTOS OR PENS?

I remember watching the New York City Marathon one particular year. The race was broadcast live, and, even in Canada, I got to tune in on TV. This marathon is one of the most globally watched races in the world. A media celebrity ran that race and she took pictures all along the way which were beamed around the globe.

Why did she do that? "To capture the moment", she explained, after crossing the finish line and falling to her knees, tired—yet happy.

I get it. We take photos on holidays and weddings. Or in the case of the celebrity in this story, during her first and only marathon.

> Photos do not record our thoughts and feelings. Use your pen!

But I also believe we should record more of our thoughts—photos do not do that.

One benefit of running daily is that my best ideas get recorded using my favorite fountain pen.

I make it a point to enter some of my experiences in my journal after the majority of my runs, because I have found that motion indeed creates emotion to paraphrase Tony Robbins. I store my experiences and insights away like a squirrel hides precious nuts to be returned to at a later time.

"Is there any science to back that up?" I hear you asking me.

Yes…indeed there is. Maud Purcell, LCSW, CEAP explained the science behind the health benefits of journaling in PsychCentral. (See <u>www.psychcentral.com/lib/the-health-benefits-of</u> journaling/.)

The bottom line is that journaling helps us to clarify our thoughts and feelings; we get to know ourselves better; it reduces stress; we are able to solve problems more effectively and it helps us to resolve disagreements with others.

I "buy" that research, hook, line and sinker!

The wise and articulate Oscar Wilde, a famous 19th Century playwright wrote, "I never travel without my diary. One should always have something sensational to read on the train."

Even if there were no research or no Oscar Wilde, I would stand by my story —record memories on paper. And if you insist, don't use a pen, certainly not a leaking and ink-staining fountain pen, but use your laptop or electronic device of choice.

- **We can choose how we record memories. May I suggest you add a pen to your photo.**

TWENTY POSITIVES

To recover from all the hard work involved in training for marathons I love to spend time reading a good book.

I recently read a book on how to sustain a happy marriage. As an endurance athlete and a runner who has decided to be consistent by running every day, as long as the Grace of God keeps me alive, I am always keen to learn more about the topic of sustaining efforts. My running afforded me personal experience of how persistence pays high dividends over time.

The book *Eight Dates* explains that a healthy relationship has a ratio of 20 positives to every negative. For example, one negative may be where the husband forgets to take out the trash, but there are at least 20 positives left in the mind of the spouse who still loves him.

By the way, when the couple engages in conflict the author, John Gottman, a well-respected psychologist and founder of the Love Lab in Seattle, claims that the ratio drops to five positives for every negative.

In another book *Resilient,* psychologist Rick Hanson explains why the mind is like Velcro for the bad things that happen to us and like Teflon for the good parts of living. Why do we remember the bad more easily than the good?

In this lifetime we will experience many ups and down. It is a given. The last time I put in a long-distance call to heaven, I was told that the script is not available; that we are not asked to give our permission before we suffer, and that life is what is happening to us —regardless of what we may want. I have heard reframes saying that life is that which happens *for us* rather than *to us*. This is only true if we respond after something negative happens rather than react and get bitter.

We will never run out of opportunities to look at the positive first and foremost. However, we grow when we also learn from negative experiences.

As I age and slow down, and as I look at the picture on the wall in my office of me finishing the Boston Marathon when I was still young and fast, I decided to live by the 20:1 principle. It means that I always look for ways to reframe things in a way that there are 20 positives for each negative. Why don't you join me today and do the same?

Choose one area that matters the most to you and ensure the 20:1 principle is cultivated daily.

- **Choose to live by the meanwhile principle. It says that there is indeed a negative somewhere, but meanwhile, I will count all the other positives.**

FALL IN LOVE

Running may not appeal to a very wide audience—even if it is easy to do anywhere, and anytime, at any pace—but one thing that running daily has done *for me* is that it has allowed me to fall in love.

I am totally in love with life. I subscribe to the notion that when we love life, life will love us back.

One of my mentors and role models lived in New York City. He wrote a number of New York Times bestseller books and answered the calling of teaching millions all over the world how to always think positive by seeing a reframe of the seemingly constant nagging negatives. It is easier to love life—even in the deep darkness of negative situations—when one pro-actively cultivates the art of positive thinking.

Because his default-setting was that of being a negative thinker most of his early life, he decided to write a book with the title *The Power of Positive Thinking*.

In one of his books, he told a story of taking a ferry one evening from New Jersey to Manhattan. It was already very dark. His mother was with him as they took the short ride toward the bright, tall skylines of Manhattan.

My mentor, feeling sorry for himself once again, was melancholic and did not notice what his mother saw—the romance of tall skyscrapers lit up and reflecting on the surface of the river. She noticed some thin fog patches and felt the cool breeze on her wrinkled face.

> His mother reminded him to develop his eyes for
> spotting the romance in the commonplaces of life.

When he complained about his life, his mother passionately reminded him in no uncertain terms to develop his eyes better. She told him to get better at spotting the romance in the commonplaces of life.

That story, as told by Dr. Norman Vincent Peale, resonated with me.

In fact, whenever I run in New York City it is my habit to admire all the tall buildings towering over the congested, busy sidewalks below. It is one of the most beautiful man-made "jungles" in the world.

Over and over, I have fallen in love with life itself during my runs—always grateful for the opportunity to move at my own pace; always glad I have eyes to see, a nose to smell, and ears to hear. I have tried hard to keep my soul clear, my spiritual life simple, and my mind on the many positives I tend to so easily take for granted.

Sometimes we all miss the commonplace. The mundane is so easily taken for granted. In Zen, the masters teach us how to establish what they call a "Beginner's Mind."

My host at the cottage by the lake where we stayed at a few summers ago told a story of how he was ten years old when he started to come to the lake. He inherited a cozy, small, and tidy place right next to the lake. His wife is a master at decorating their small but ideally situated home.

As soon as we stepped onto their property we were met by an atmosphere of tranquility.

I asked Ken if he thought about how lucky he was to be living in what they now call "Our little paradise by the lake." He admitted there was a time they took it for granted...until visitor after visitor told them the same thing independently: "You are living in a little paradise by the lake."

Ever since those moments Ken sees his place through beginner's eyes. But what if Ken never saw the potential of his little paradise by the lake? I may not have been the beneficiary of his vision.

- **Life is short; do what you enjoy and remember to look at the commonplace along the way…moment-by-moment-by-moment.**

OUR CHOICES

During one of my runs I listened to a podcast. I heard a story I shall always remember.

It was the story of a man who was in quite a hurry. He was running late and to add insult to injury, he had to stop at a railway crossing to wait for an exceptionally long train to pass. While waiting, a beggar approached his stationary car and asked for some kindness.

Fortunately, our friend obliged and though the amount was small, and the time was brief, there was a sacred momentary connection between two humans, soul to soul, heart to heart and eyes to eyes.

Afterwards the driver of the vehicle reflected that maybe it all was a set-up. Was it a test? Was it an opportunity to choose kindness instead of selfishness?

I have heard some New Age teachers teach that every negative is there by design so that we can choose to grow and be kind. Of course, the *real* reasons for negative situations—moments where we experience what we did not ask for or wanted, moments of unsatisfactoriness—can be debated.

However, it is hard to prove definitively, without a shadow of doubt, that this reframe is indeed accurate. We will never know for sure. It takes a measure of deep faith.

Some scientists may call faith a form of observation bias, but what cannot be debated is that we always have a choice.

When I recently considered the matter of choice, inspired by the story of the man in a hurry getting stopped by a train in order to choose kindness, I could not help but remind myself that the stories we make up in our minds are simply *our* stories. Like the man who carried a hammer, we too look for nails.

During some of my runs during election years I tend to keep myself up to speed by listening to podcasts that summarize the latest about the game of mudslinging and insults—also known as politics.

I became interested in politics when I was a teenager. During those times, politicians were also called public servants. The public's best interests came first. That was then, and this is now.

At the time of this writing times have changed. The "servant" part is seen by some skeptics as a golden opportunity to self-serve by benefitting from spending the hard-earned money of taxpayers in ways that are not exactly skillful. When over-spending is renamed as "investing" one can tell which way the wind is blowing.

It may even appear that some politicians fail to be considerate of the monumental tax burden they are selfishly passing on to our children. The same people who want life to be fair, forget to be fair to the next generation.

This is not a book about politics, but these are the things I ponder when I run. I am authentic in sharing my thoughts generated while running with you.

The good news is that what has not changed about democracy is the opportunity to vote. In most democratic counties this takes place every four years or so. But every day we get to vote when it comes to wellness choices. We can vote for ourselves or vote against ourselves by how we choose to eat, exercise, rest, or think.

All of us are invited daily to make thousands of choices. Although I have no regrets that I have chosen to run daily and continue to do marathons for as long as my Higher Power allows me good health, I realize there is so much more to life than physical exercise.

I was told that a man went to the bank and ordered new cheques. The teller told him that at that specific bank there was an option to write a few inspirational words close to the area where the signature was meant to be written. The client told the teller, "I would like to have these words printed close to my signature: *Remember what is really important.*"

The poet and philosopher Rumi once said, "Worldly power means nothing. Only the unsayable jewelled inner life matters." So often in our Western culture we focus on sex, sloth, silver, and self…when in truth these are to play important roles, but they will never be as important as the inner jewels mentioned by Rumi.

Physical wellness happens when we balance our choices skillfully and in wholesome ways. When we choose to react quickly it often ends up producing negative outcomes. Instead, look for skillful ways to respond by cultivating a jewelled inner life.

Negative things may happen regardless of our explanations as to why they happened, but this I know for sure, having considered it carefully and diligently over many miles of running:

- **We all get multiple invitations to choose how we want to respond or react.**

FREEDOM

There is a song I heard many moons ago. It left quite a mark in my memory. I believe the artist may have been Kris Kristofferson. The words were, "Freedom's just another word for nothing left to lose."

My own definition of freedom is where we can honestly say we have peace of mind regardless of circumstances. For example, outside a Buddhist Temple were these words: *Do not find peace here. Find it everywhere.*

Freedom from frustrations depends on my peace of mind.

I am reminded that peace is already possible and there for us to take, but it is something like a tan—one has to consistently cultivate it. In order to maintain a tan, one must go back into the sun often.

This is where people miss the mark and fail to get to the finish line: once they feel like they achieved peace they expect it to last. This is delusional. Delusions cause us to suffer.

We all feel happy and content when life works out the way we want it to. Satisfactoriness is what many seek. But as we know by now a constant state of satisfaction is impossible. When we get too attached to the notion that peace of mind is only possible once we are satisfied with our health, looks, fitness, weight, relationship, finances, and general well-being, then we are at risk of being trapped in a state of insufficient peace of mind.

One of my teachers is Dr. Jerry Jampolsky, the founder of Attitudinal Healing. One of the 12 Principles of Attitudinal Healing is principle number eight:

I can choose and direct myself to be peaceful inside regardless of what is happening outside.

So many factors have to come together in order to finish running a distance of 26.2 miles in a time that matches a goal that is set before the race starts. One has to consider factors such as heat, wind, hills, the number of other runners who may slow one down, hydration, sleep-deprivation, weight,, and a number of other variables not under one's control.

Having completed over 100 marathons taught me this simple but timeless truth—easy to say but hard to do—

- **I can choose if I want to be peaceful inside regardless of what is happening to me.**

THE PAUSE?

One thing I learned as a doctor is that all my patients get an invitation. Some are given bad news and then they are invited. Some are overweight and then get invited.

In fact, all of us have to decide when the road forks, which fork to take; how to answer the invitations we get over a lifetime.

Here is a Universal Invitation: will you respond, or will you react?

When our bodies respond to a medication, that is good news. Reacting to a medication? Not good news at all.

Every person who breathes on a mirror in the mornings and sees it fog up knows they are still alive, and they get to choose. Am I going to be happy today and make peace my only goal or not?

React or respond?

> After every stimulus there needs to be a pause…then a response.

I have been told that after every stimulus there needs to be a pause…then a response.

Driving down a freeway where I live, I notice a recent increase of middle fingers—people are cut off and by default immediately out comes that long middle digit. People are tail-gated and irritated, and they move over ...then the middle finger is promptly waved around with disgust.

That is not skillful. Its reacting. It is not responding. It is bad for your blood pressure and your immunity. You may feel good for a moment, but on a cellular level your mitochondria are working overtime to cope. Sort of like a cell phone or computer that heats up, trying to function properly under tough situations. Or a furnace that works overtime when it is minus 40 degrees.

In marathon running—real marathons and navigating the marathon of grieving the loss of a child—I have learned skillful ways to conserve energy. One must become skillful at responding rather than reacting in every situation in life.

One hundred marathons are behind me. Yet the journey was more important than the finish line. What I learned was not so much that the finish line is the goal—the goal is to learn along the way when life gives us what we did not want or expect.

I have observed this important lesson—a quite simple lesson indeed, yet not easy to do moment-by-moment-by moment—

- **When the road forks...first pause before you choose which fork to take.**

LAUGHTER

I was about three miles from the finish line. My body was aching but, my mind was set on getting to the end of yet another windy Las Vegas marathon. The third year in a row of strong gusts of winds.

For the third year in a row, I discovered that luck is that which happens when preparation and opportunity meet. God knows—and so does my wife and family—I trained hard, extremely hard, for three years in a row, but failed to meet my goals, thanks to Mother Nature who had other plans.

Hard work did not pay off because the opportunity was missing. Fate was stacked against me. For the third year in a row, I encountered head winds. All three years there was no wind the day *before* the marathon, and the day *after* the race…no wind as in the leaves of the palm trees along the strip just hanging limp and hardly moving at all. Lighting a candle would never be easier on the days before and after the marathon.

Little did I know that just before the end of the windy race I was going to engage in internal jogging. At least that is what some psychologists call laughter.

I could have cried but ended up laughing so hard I had to stop to compose myself. As we all know there are times when we laugh so hard, we can hardly breathe—a bit like being tickled…we just want the stimulus to stop.

Here is what unfolded with three miles left—just before the internal jogging began. I clearly heard a male runner closing in on me, swearing like a sailor. Every other word started with the letter F and rhymed with "duck." When he passed me, I discovered we were in the same boat: he too tried to qualify for the Boston Marathon, but just like me, three years in a row, headwinds thwarted his efforts. By mile 23 he had it. His mouth expressed his heart—he was ticked to say the least.

This is what I learned as I reflect a few years later: life has a habit of giving us what we do not want, but it is what we got. It is so…it cannot be otherwise.

We look back, and as Dale Carnegie said, we try to saw sawdust. Instead, we may choose to let it go. It is so. Sometimes it is what it is; it cannot be otherwise.

I tried hard—three years in a row—to run a fast-enough marathon to get me back to Boston a third time. I was up hours before sunrise, running in sleet and snow and slipping on ice; I went to bed early and skipped very entertaining TV shows to get at least eight hours of sleep; I watched every bit of food I swallowed mindfully, to arrive for three years in a row at the ideal weight for those Vegas marathons.

I did my part in preparing; the opportunity did not arrive. Mother Nature foiled it every year in the exact same way. Destiny spoke loud and clear.

Since then, I am learning that if I do my best, I need to let go of the outcome.

Humor every so often releases the endorphins we so desperately need to stay calm and peaceful inside, regardless of what is happening outside. If the internal jogging part is true, then technically all of us are joggers.

I know…its way easier said than done. To do this more often requires deep wisdom. We only have two choices: either accept that we do not control everything and move on, or cling to the idea we control outcomes and try harder.

When we make the latter unwise choice, I have observed, we suffer. In fact, when we are sinking it is unwise to cling to what we think is a raft while it is not a raft, but something else.

- **Cultivate a deep self–compassion and understanding that some things we control, while others we can never in a million years control or change.**

SEE FOR YOURSELF

Contentment under all circumstances is possible. It may not be frequent, but it is possible with mindful cultivation.

I did not say that, but learned about this concept from a man, now known as the Buddha, who lived 2,600 years ago. He explained that peace is indeed possible, even though we may face numerous negatives.

> Many times in life we do not get what we chose or wanted, but it is what we got—like it or not.

As one of my teachers, Sylvia Boorstein, wrote, and I am paraphrasing her words a bit: "Many times in life we do not get what we chose or wanted, but it is what we got—like it or not. So now what?"

The Buddha also said you do not have to believe him but invited you and me to stay open and see for ourselves if contentment is possible—at least for the majority of our lives.

The Buddha taught that there is a way out of suffering. The simplicity of his teaching is such that 2,600 years later, it still helps millions around the world to find contentment.

But he did not force people to believe what he taught. Instead, he offered this suggestion: "Come and see for yourself. Try it. Play with it. Find out if it works for you." (Again, I am paraphrasing the Buddha's ideas the way

I understand and interpret them.) It is like trying on a pair of shoes or a coat…make sure it fits properly and if not then don't use it.

During my runs I get to choose if I want to listen to nature or wise teachers on podcasts. Those are my experiences, but all of us have to see for ourselves. When we do that, we are more likely to deepen our beliefs and strengthen our mindsets.

I tend to balance all options and end up with a middle way—a bit of all in the correct dosages.

In Zen there is a teaching that less is more.

So here is what the Buddha taught me and continues to teach me when I listen to a podcast called "Dharmaseed":

- We all struggle and suffer; nobody is immune.
- One of the main reasons we suffer is that we choose to hold on too tightly to what we thirst for. It is also known as clinging. (For example, most of us mindlessly cling to the idea that things can stay the same, when in fact, life is all about adjusting to change.)
- There is a path that leads us away from suffering. It is like a prescription to heal a disease.
- That path is the Eight-fold path: it involves the right view, skillful thoughts, concentration, meditation, the right speech, the right actions, skillful effort, and the right livelihood.

Yet the above approach reminds me of a seven-foot tall man. Imagine this man looking at life from that high while others have a lower perspective. It will be absurd to insist all others must also have a seven-foot tall view. The point is simply that we all are different, and all the things mentioned in this book have no certainty to work for you the way they worked for me.

We are given the beautiful privilege to choose which principles resonate the best. Make sure the shoe is not just your size but that it actually fits properly. See for yourself. Then run or walk in ways that serve you well.

We all are different yet we all have the same basic needs—to be fed, to sleep, to eat, to be safe, to connect with others, to get along with ourselves, and to know why we are here on this planet. Maslow called the latter "Self-Actualization" —which is when people are true to their own calling, free from the opinion of others and living a life of purpose and meaning.

- **When you buy a shoe that is your size you still have to try it on to make sure it fits.**

DIRECT EXPERIENCE

My wife, Corinne, gave birth to four beautiful healthy babies and I was there every time, next to her as her partner, husband and friend, to welcome one girl and three boys to this planet. In one of the photos taken just after dawn—soon after the birth of our first son Matthew--I am wearing a Boston Marathon running jacket and beaming a smiling, happy face to the world.

Corinne also smiled, but she showed fatigue as only a woman can know.

My marathon was nothing compared to Corinne's as a woman in labor. Four times she did this amazing sacrifice to allow another human being the opportunity of entering this world.

Although I was always present, one thing is for sure: I have no personal experience of pain related to childbirth.

> And so it is in life itself. Unless we experience pain and suffering, we may never know what we are capable of enduring.

And so, it is in life itself. Unless we experience pain and suffering, we may never know what we are capable of enduring.

I have experienced an intellectual and philosophical knowing from reading wise words in Scriptures and ancient texts or carefully listening to wise teachers. But it was during my deepest mental marathons of suffering where I got to a place of *gnosis*.

Gnosis is a Greek word referring to a knowing based on experience. It is indeed the best teacher.

Before I had children, I saw a number of families where a child and the family struggled to cope with inattention—so called Attention Deficit Disorder. My youngest son Ben was diagnosed diagnosed at age six with this condition. Only then did I experience gnosis, a knowing, an understanding, a higher degree of empathy of how families are impacted by ADD.

- **To experience something first-hand is to understand truly and deeply.**

CHILDREN

A person is a person, no matter how small.

—Dr. Seuss

The greatest legacy one can pass on to one's children and grandchildren
is not money or other material things
accumulated in one's life, but rather
a legacy of character and faith.

—Billy Graham

Children make our life important.

—Erma Bombeck

BE A FLY ON THE WALL

Not so long ago I was waiting to catch a flight, not to a marathon in the USA, but to learn about healthy ways to fuel my body with plant-based foods. I was excited to learn more about the many long-term health benefits of *only* eating a whole food, plant-based diet. Before I boarded the flight, however, a child at the airport became my first teacher on this trip. And it had nothing to do with food.

I did not mean to listen in or be a fly on the wall or a parrot on a shoulder, but I could not help it. I heard the conversation between a loving father and his six-year-old boy.

It all happened behind me. I heard it all. The father was timing his son who was aiming to run from where the dad was sitting to an imaginary line about twenty feet away, and then making a rapid U–turn back to the dad.

"Ready…steady…GO!" I heard the dad call out, just before his son took off like a rocket. Seven seconds later the little guy was back, asking the father who was looking down at the stopwatch on his phone, "Dad how long was that?" the little fellow enquired.

His face lit up when he heard "seven seconds" coming from his dad, who enthusiastically added, "You broke your record by 0.5 seconds!"

"Let's do it again!" shouted this energetic young runner with much enthusiasm. And he did it almost again. Soon after his dad said, "Ready… steady…GO!" the father added, "Wait! False start …you started to run before I said GO."

Such an honest man…such a great teacher…such a wise man who did not check his email and ignore his son, but instead played with his youngster in all "seriousness".

I looked around and saw I was not the only fly on this wall. I saw many strangers with bemused smiles, on their faces. We all saw this family having fun, sharing a moment of special bonding.

This father knew what to do *and* did it. He engaged his son at a level of a six-year-old. Some parents know to do that more often, but they put it off for later. They know what to do but do the opposite.

This young runner and his dad taught me a valuable lesson that day. It was too late for me, but not too late to share with the parents of babies who put their trust in me as a pediatrician.

- **When you know what to do…do it. Sometimes there are no second chances.**

BICYCLES

Training to run 26.2 miles takes lots of time and effort. This story shows how almost every run has a lesson. Like life itself, every day brings the potential of personal growth and new insights. When we are curious by nature, we see things which may be obvious, but which can be easily missed.

It was a warm day and only a slight breeze stirred colorful flowers along my path. Lilly white butterflies floated back and forth over deep green meadows, almost dancing to the tune of a happy song. I was caught up in thoughts of deep gratitude for being able to soak in the many joys of being in nature.

It was then that I heard an excited child's voice behind me. *"Ring, ring... sorry my bell does not work."* A young girl passed me at a safe distance, and soon after that her brother, who used his bell instead of saying *"Ring, Ring"*, passed me too, asking the little sister *"Do you want me to buy you a bell?"*

On another occasion my wife and I were running next to a huge body of water. A father and his five-year old were cycling toward us and the timing of their conversation was special.

A few men were at the edge of the lake holding on to their fishing rods and staring motionlessly at the water ahead of them. They were as quiet as mice while just sitting and seemingly doing nothing.

The little boy asked his father, "Dad do the fishermen bring magazines to read or do they just sit and watch the water?"

The father with a wide grin on his face passed us by and I heard him tell his son, "No they don't read any magazines. They just sit and watch the water. That is what fishermen do."

As a pediatrician with close to forty years of experience, seeing how children grow and progress through the various seasons of growing up, I must admit a certain bias. I love kids and the reasons are many. But one thing stands out:

—They tend to be very authentic when they are young.

Teenagers have taught me a lot over the years, but it is the young, unspoiled, non-jaded, and present-moment-awareness preschoolers that taught me the most.

The little fellow who rang his bell and asked his sister if she wanted him to buy her a bell taught me that there are some very caring people on this planet. How often do we notice a need and ignore it?

- **Learn from kids. We think we are there to teach them; the reality is that we can learn much *from* them.**

OVERTAKEN

The flight which brought me back from Las Vegas landed in Canada about eight hours after I finished a marathon on the famous Strip. Usually after one passes through customs it is a very quick process to get into the rest of the airport terminal and then to the taxi stand. I was in a rush when, suddenly, I heard a woman's voice calling out my name.

It happened to be a nurse who used to bring her children to me about ten years ago. I lost contact with the family and was pleasantly surprised to meet this mom again.

"How are the kids?" I asked.

"They are great!" she answered and then she also added, "As a matter of fact, my oldest daughter just ran her first marathon today in Vegas." Upon further questioning I discovered that my former patient and I ran in the same marathon and she finished a few minutes ahead of me. We never knew we were in the same race. By now she was in her mid-twenties and I was glad that at age 55, thirty years her senior, she only beat me by a few minutes! Perhaps I was not that slow after all!

I did slow down toward the end I remembered. For sure she must have overtaken me without realizing she did that to her "old" doctor?

A more dramatic and obvious case of being overtaken happened when a twelve-year-old kid passed by me *really* fast during a local marathon. Later his photo was in the newspaper with a caption explaining that he was one of the youngest and fastest marathon runners in Canada.

As a scientist I am always curious to get the correct facts, so I researched what science had to say about the safety and health of letting such young athletes cover a marathon distance. The bottom-line is that age 12 is too young. And yet the parents, according to the newspaper, were proud that they allowed their child to pursue his dreams.

I pondered the wisdom of the parents. On the one hand it was their decision, but on the other hand as a physician I could not help but wonder about the future health of that young marathoner.

A recent photo in another newspaper showed a picture of a Boeing coming in to land at the same airport I landed at after the Vegas marathon. The photographer must have used a telephoto lens which distorted the perspectives and thus caused an optical illusion making the city look as if its edges were right next to the airport. It was a distorted picture which would deceive most people unfamiliar with reality.

That photo caused me to wonder how often in life we look at what is real and yet perceive it incorrectly. Distortions can deceive.

Perception changes the way we interpret life. The right view —accurately seeing what must be seen—leads to the right actions and right thoughts. What we say depends on our perceptions. It seems so simple and yet hard to do.

My regular morning mindfulness meditation has helped me to set time aside to take what Joseph Campbell called, "The Hero's Journey." It is the journey of reflecting and going *inside*. I am always keen to review my motives for doing what I do. As Plato reminded us many centuries ago: an unexamined life is not worth living.

When we go inside, we need to be reminded to stay truthful and accurate. I was told that denial stands for "Don't even notice I am lying." Another person once told me that denial is not a river in Egypt. It was funny at the time, but to truly cultivate the right perception about things that are important is no laughing matter.

I was not paying attention to the fact that I was overtaken by a former patient at one marathon yet at another marathon I easily noticed when a 12-year-old child overtook me. The first kind of being overtaken did not bother me, but the second kind of being overtaken by a young kid did bother me. I was concerned he may get injured. Of course, his motives and his parents' motives are their business, but I honestly wondered about the wisdom of letting such a young child run a marathon.

As I look back to the above stories of other runners overtaking me, I was reminded that:

- **We do not always know the motives of others. We can only focus on how we perceive things and trust that others will know their own true motives.**

ANIMALS

Dogs are our link to paradise.
They don't know evil or jealousy or discontent.

—Milan Kundera

An animal's eyes have the power
to speak a great language.

—Martin Buber

Until one has loved an animal,
a part of one's soul remains Unawakened.

—Anatole France

A DOG AT O'HARE

I was waiting by a curb for my ride to arrive at one of the world's busiest airports. People were coming and going like ants. Just when I got tired of waiting, wondering if the driver of my Uber ride got lost, my spirit was uplifted by man's best friend.

A sparkling white Mercedes slowly came to a halt a few feet from where I was standing. In the back seat was a medium sized, fluffy white dog, with a tail wagging so fast it almost became a blur. This little guy was about to jump out of his skin when he spotted his master depositing a suitcase in the trunk of the fancy car.

I did not see if the master got his face licked when he slid into the front passenger seat, but I am guessing he did. No doubt this cute fluffy dog was a true spirit lifter.

Unconditional love heals—always.

I have seen it at airports and at marathon finish lines when a loved one is welcomed by a family member. Often a furry friend with a wagging tail and bright eyes waits at the finish line while carefully following every move of the runners getting closer, certain that the next one will be his owner.

> I often wonder what would happen if someone made a movie about humans who have tails and who drool.

I often wonder what would happen if someone made a movie about humans who have tails and who drool. Would it help us know better if we are welcome or not?

Imagine this: you are trying to impress your date at a restaurant. All goes well until your neighbors get their nice-smelling and good-looking food delivered by a friendly waiter. You cannot help looking at the delicious dish. You start to drool all over the place. This is not good in the eyes of your new date. You leave the table to clean your face…but your tail is between your legs. You are in the dog box!

- **Be glad you do not drool or have a tail…but imitate a dog by showing enthusiasm and unconditional love.**

LIONS AT TOP OF STAIRS

At the top of the stairs, leading up to my bedroom and the shower, hangs a huge photo.

It is a stunning photo of two lions—a mother holding her son close to her majestic, rippling, muscular body. The artist chose to call this wonderful photo, "You are my son."

Usually when a marathon runner races there is no time to pause; it is always full steam ahead. There were some races out of the hundred plus marathons I completed where I simply ran with no particular agenda; no urgency; no goal; no intention other than to be fully present in the moment and take one step at a time—- all the way from the start to the finish, 26.2 miles later.

But given the powerful image this photo radiates, it always causes me to pause and reflect.

Obviously, the strength, grace, and courage radiating from the image of a mother lion and her baby encourage me to stay strong and courageous. The close connection between these two creatures reminds me to pay attention to whom I want to stay intimately connected to in the days ahead.

Pictures are indeed worth 1000 words.

For some of us it may be a photo to remind us of the Hawaiian expression *Kuleana,* which I am told can be loosely translated to "What is yours to do?"

Perhaps yours to do is to be more courageous; to be more present; to be less intense; to be more self-compassionate; to deliver the various gifts the Creator has put in you—not so much for your own ego, but rather to be able to honestly say in the mornings, "How may I serve?"

One of my all-time favorite stories is from the book, *The Lion the Witch and the Wardrobe*, written by C.S Lewis. This extremely popular book is really a story about a metaphor. It is about a Creator and about us—mere mortals who always must know that we are just *that*: mortal.

As much as we think we can control our own breath and heartbeat…we don't.

Instead, we are all brothers and sisters, interconnected, dependant on an Invisible Intelligence for waking us up the next day from our, hopefully, deep and restful sleep.

So, although we are similar but never the same, I use the image of the lions at the top of our stairs to remind me to always be courageous; and to stay courageous. That is actually the hard part—sustaining such an attitude.

We face losses; we face the unexpected vicissitudes of life; we face uncertainty; we grieve when loved ones move on to another realm ahead of us; we learn how to manage skillfully emotions and feelings that, even when they come and go, would want us to believe that they are there to stay.

So, in the end we all are artists, and chefs—we create. We create a picture by living a life on purpose. We seek our unique Kuleana. Once we know what is ours to do…we do it. We do it one step at a time—just like running marathons.

So here is a question I often ask myself at the top of the stairs:

- **If your life were a picture, would it cause some to pause and feel the energy it radiates?**

SAGE

Most of my daily runs are early in the day.

These are the times when I aim to reflect and plan ahead. It's my playtime. It is a time for going inside and discovering what I value and how I may serve those who need what I have to offer.

I had a friend who insisted on joining me as often as possible. This friend was not always ready to go on long runs before sunrise, but later in the day, as soon as I arrived home, this friend met me— without fail—every day at the door to our house.

I was followed upstairs. My friend watched me change into running clothes. I was stalked, but as I close my eyes remembering her, now long gone, I can still see her enthusiasm—manifested in a wildly-wagging-tail. She always begged to go on a run with me. I wish I never left her at home... but I did a few times.

The runs I allowed her to join me on are sweet memories stored away somewhere in my mind. I can even now close my eyes and reflect back. I can feel her pulling on the leash.

And when I open my eyes, I know she is gone. I am thankful for what we had. She uplifted my spirits so often. I got upgraded emotionally, mentally and in many other ways when she came running with me or even when she sat next to me afterwards, looking me in the eyes with a deep and penetrating stare as if to say *"I see you and thanks for allowing us to do this together. I love you very much."* And did she ever teach me. Not about love. But about *unconditional* love.

Now that she is gone, I miss her. I wish I said yes to her more often. At the time I was worried she would slow me down. I took her company for granted until we discovered a tumor on one of her legs.

Sage was my first and only dog during my running career. I suspect she is my last dog. I have been told to get another dog, but right now I am simply not ready for more pain to come when that dog dies. I am not alone as the following story will show.

Once, toward the end of Sage's life while she could still move a bit, we got stopped by a stranger. He simply wanted to touch her soft coat and get his face licked, basking in the way she gave love unconditionally even while in much pain.

I shall never forget the tears in his eyes. After he got down to Sage's level and made eye contact, he stood up and wiped big tears from his eyes. He went on to explain, "She reminds me so much of my own dog."

I asked him "How old is your dog?" Before he answered there was an exceptionally long pause.

"My dog died twenty years ago," he said softly. "I still miss her so very much."

When I told him about Sage's sad future, that she was in the end stages of her battle with cancer, he cried some more. We cried together there next to a stream where Sage often wanted to stop on runs in order to get a few gulps of fresh water.

They say that feeling our emotions rather than swallowing them is healing. I once heard the saying that when we swallow our emotions our stomach keeps score and ultimately the emotions cause a pain in the butt.

That day with Sage and a stranger, who loved her the moment he saw her, reminded me to:

- **Make the most of every opportunity. Be thankful for what you had…rather than focusing on your loss.**

NATURE

Heaven is under our feet as well as over
our heads.

—-Henry David Thoreau

Nature does not hurry.
Yet everything is accomplished.

—-Lao Tzu

MORNING SKIES

One of the great benefits of running at dawn is to witness how a new day is about to unfold.

Not so long ago I ran just before sunrise and the direction of my run was toward the west. In the running community we call some runs "out-and-back" runs, meaning we run the first half in one direction, and then turn around to complete the second half in the opposite direction.

On that particular crisp morning I was stunned by what I saw as I made a switch from west to east: the sun was low on the horizon, the clouds were colorful, and what was even more amazing is how the sun's rays landed on my running path.

I took a photo, shared it on Facebook, and saw later why so many people liked that photo. It was as if one had to only run a few yards forward in order to touch a bright and long ray of sunlight falling at my feet; the photo awakened thoughts of an unusual mystical experience. No words could capture that moment of an orb gracing the skies.

Ironically, when I got home after my run, I read these words from a book written by Dr. Peale (*The Amazing Results of Positive Thinking*) where he skillfully used words to paint a picture of what he saw from his living room one morning at dawn:

> *I went into the living room and looked at the glorious morning sky. It suddenly occurred to me that Emerson was right when he said: "The sky is the daily bread of the soul."*

Our apartment faces west, overlooking Central Park, an area in the heart of the city, four miles long and one-half mile wide. The sky that morning was like a gigantic fireplace, with flames shooting up over the city. There was a soft blanket of broken clouds overhead and, across the park, windows were golden as they reflected the rising sun. The whole city was as still as an etching. The air was clear as crystal. The snow was clean and fresh and sparkling. Suddenly I felt a strong instinct to pray and the prayer became one of joy and exhilaration. It was an unforgettable experience. That day was a wonderful day.

Running at dawn the past three decades brought me the same wonderful days Dr. Peale described here.

Because I live so far from the Equator, in winter the sun actually rises not in the east, but in the southeast and it sets not in the west, but in the southwest. Nevertheless, every dawn is a gift like manna—good for that day only.

At dawn, when the morning skies light up, I usually experience a deep sense of gratitude for that moment and I know that:

- **The sky is the daily bread of the soul.**

RAINBOW RUN

One of my most popular Facebook posts ever is that of a picture taken at sunrise one morning in Chicago. I used to never take my smartphone on runs, fretting that if I fell during a run or ended up by accident in a dark alleyway and got mugged, that would mean then end of my phone!

But on this particular morning I got woken up by heavy rain. What seemed to be a gazillion drops of rain pounded against my hotel window. I was in no mood to do what I usually do at dawn—run.

But after going through my usual 30 minute morning pre-running-routine, I was ready to face the rain…only to discover it had stopped.

A few minutes later I found myself heading out toward the east, invigorated by the noise of many jets above, descending from the sky as they were approaching O'Hare airport…also heading east.

When it was time to turn back, I saw dark western skies. *More rain* I thought. The thought had hardly crossed my mind when I was stopped dead in my tracks, spotting one of the biggest, longest, double rainbows I have ever witnessed in my 60 plus years on this planet.

In our journey to be more resilient, it is wise to remember the reframe method of coping with what we do not appreciate. It is so easy to be discontent when we are in a state of unsatisfactoriness. But there is always a plus somewhere.

One of my teachers reminded me a minus is simply a matter of knowing where to draw the vertical line. When we do that, a minus becomes a plus.

When I worked with the publishers of my first book, *Moving Forward,* we had to decide on the cover. I had no doubt as to how the cover should look: a rainbow by the ocean.

I love water and especially being next to the vast ocean...but I also know that symbolically a rainbow represents faithfulness. I have been the humble recipient of the faithfulness of my Creator over many decades. Over all the years of running—-an activity that is not so much about the running itself, but rather an activity which sustains my own resilience when I need to face the roller-coaster-rides of life itself—I have not for one single day taken running for granted.

- **When looking at rainbows don't think of the pot of gold at the end; think of the symbolism it represents—the faithfulness of a Creator.**

LEAVES AND LILACS

My run this morning smelled nice. It took me along a route where at the start of summer, I encountered beautiful lilacs.

Where I live lilacs do not last long enough. Maybe two weeks at best. Thus, the brevity of their lives makes them extra special as they bring us their bright colors and stimulating fragrances.

One day I updated my journal using my favorite fountain pen. I sat by the kitchen table after doing my second run on a gorgeous day in summer. Next to me were some lilacs in a vase. The fragrance filled the room. I was in paradise. The stress I was facing became temporarily muted.

Suddenly I was reminded to soak in all I could while I had it.

My favorite book in Scriptures is Ecclesiastes where we are reminded in chapter three that there is an appointed time for everything, and that death is ever present. After the lilacs were long gone, summer abruptly ended; autumn arrived.

Fall is one of my most favourite seasons because it is a lull where we brace ourselves for a protracted, upcoming cold winter.

During a recent fall run I smelled the smell of fallen leaves and heard them rustle under my feet. It is a very distinct and unique smell. I found myself actually pausing for one minute, interrupting my steady strides, with the intention to remember what it feels like to be fully alive.

It is so easy to overlook the brevity of life. But because I am a student of mindfulness methods which are targeted to help us remember and to become more aware, I was glad that my sense of smell stopped me in my tracks. My hectic mind was tamed by fragrances during this run.

The good news is that even when lilacs are not in bloom, there are always flowers with great fragrances for purchase at the friendly flower shop around the corner. And thus, I am reminded often to place these flowers close to where I eat and write:

- **Use flowers to bring you mental nourishment—even when it snows outside.**

HELIOTHERAPY

In Greek the word "Helios" is used to describe the sun.

Heliotherapy leaves its mark much deeper than one's skin if one allows it. Sunshine can sting or soothe. I choose heliotherapy's soothing side anytime. I choose it often and get my best energy from sunshine. I do not need a functional MRI to prove that my brain is far happier in the sun than under the incessant cover of morbidly dark-grey, gloomy skies.

In fact, I like heliotherapy so much that if someone were to give me a million-dollar mansion in Vancouver or Seattle, where they refer to their rain as their "liquid sunshine", I would immediately sell the mansion and move away to a sunnier location as soon as possible.

Because I grew up in Africa, I need the sun to keep me happy. Being stuck under thick, dark clouds, week, after week, after week and needing to carry an umbrella wherever I go is *definitely* not my idea of fun at all.

Sometimes we get upgrades at hotels or from rental car companies. A different kind of upgrade for me is the mental upgrade that comes from escaping grey clouds and exchanging it for proper, bright, warm, soothing sunshine.

My dermatology friends should probably skip this part of the book, because they have seen the damage that too much sunshine can do to the human skin. Of course when a skin doctor carries a hammer, he or she will look for nails. In this case these doctors focus mostly on the risks of *any amounts* of sunshine.

A few years ago, I attended a nutrition conference in Phoenix. Although I learned much about optimal nourishment, one day I had enough of it and played hooky. Instead of sitting in a dark air-conditioned room, surrounded by keen learners taking copious amount of notes, I stepped outside and engaged in my daily hour of power.

I ran outside in Goldie-Locks sunshine—not too hot and not too cold.

As I close my eyes now, I can feel the heat, gently stroking the top of my exposed forearms. I can even smell the invigorating fragrance of freshly cut grass. I was as high as a kite from endorphins that flooded my brain. Natural highs induced by exercise and heliotherapy are the best addictions by far. They are also much healthier.

Gone from the morbid, almost constant cloudy Canadian skies, I was like a lion let out of a cage.

I was free to roam under bright blue skies for as long as I wanted to.

I feel a bit guilty though for what I said about winters in Canada. In a small town in the Rockies I recently saw a sign in a store which said, *"Forgive me for the things I said when it was winter."*

To be fair to a place called Canmore, located in the Canadian Rockies, it is not always that bad. We have a private place to retreat to every so often in Canmore. As I am typing these words I am sunbathing on the balcony, just watching an occasional cloud floating by and truly soaking in solar energy provided by seemingly endless sunshine. Today's morning run with my wife took us along a clear mountain stream and thick evergreen trees. It filled a void that is there when we are not connected to nature. Our minds were hungry and thirsty for this mountain vista.

It was indeed one of those unusual days in the mountains where I knew there would be no need to take my usual Vitamin D supplements. Fifteen minutes in nature was enough.

Recently when I rose early to do some reflection and write before my morning run, I was deeply caught up in the moment. As is the case for runners, there are times when writers, similar to runners, also get "trapped" in the zone. When this happens there is a complete loss of a sense of time. One gets fully absorbed in the present. It becomes blissful. The word "serene" or "the present" do not even come close to describing it fully. Experience alone can capture the flooded-by-good-hormones mental state.

What woke me up from my writing was the sudden burst of bright sunshine. The sun rose above the mountains to the east side of the valley where Canmore is located. Immediately I felt its warmth on my skin. Massaged—in body and mind— by sunshine; energized by light and heat; a symbolic reminder to me to bring light and warmth to others in the days ahead.

The paths of the sun from dawn to dusk are nature's ways to remind me that its timing is always perfect. The sun always speaks the loudest to me at daybreak—perhaps because it marks the start of another great day with its many opportunities.

But as the days wind down and particularly at times of sunsets, especially in Hawaii, I have noticed how many humans pause; some just sit...they sit mesmerized...and watch the sun disappear below the horizon; many pull out their phones and capture the moment. There is also something special about sunsets. It stirs something wistful in us. The end of another day with no certainty about tomorrow.

Maybe one day as we get more research, I may have to rewrite this chapter, but meanwhile like Forrest Gump, a runner who inspired me greatly, would say: "And that is all I want to say about that."

- **When you find more postcards with cloudy skies, than bright sunshine, the next time you are at a tourist shop…. please contact me.**

AFTER THE RAIN

Where I live it is not uncommon to get major downpours during our brief summers. In Texas they call these showers "frog stranglers." There is so much rain in a short time that apparently even frogs struggle to stay ahead of the curve.

Recently I was woken up by a loud clap of thunder. My cat did not like this at all and snuggled up closer. A flash of lightning suddenly brightened up the bedroom. At that moment I doubted my morning run would be safe.

But I forgot that all storms pass—some faster than others. And that particular morning, an hour after the room was lit up by lightning, my running life was lit up by the morning sun. The rain passed. The air was crisp and fresh. I paused a few seconds longer than usual and took in a deep breath of this gift delivered to me by nature.

One of the most refreshing times to connect with nature is to go for a run after the rain. It is fresh and easy on the lungs. Sometimes, totally by surprise, rainbows may colorfully populate the skies, arching high over the wide prairies and inviting me to run with determination toward one end, looking for the elusive pot of gold.

> I noticed a pattern over the last few years: every time I run after it rains the air seems to be different.

I noticed a pattern over the last few years: every time I run after it rains the air seems to be different. Different not as in cleaner, but different as in an energy level one can almost palpably sense.

It prompted me to do some research. Was I just imagining this or is it possible that after the rain is gone the air is filled with some "magical" energy field? The research confirmed that I was not imagining it. I think they call it negative ions.

Once I looked at clear blue skies at the very start of a long run, only to be trapped in a sudden fast-moving storm a short while later. I got soaked but reminded myself of Bob Marley's wisdom when he said, "Some people feel the rain. Others just get wet."

- **It is wise to feel—really feel—our experiences fully. Or we can choose to just get wet.**

POSTSCRIPT

Many times I am asked how I managed to complete over 100 marathons. My usual answer is that it all boils down to a specific mindset.

When I contemplate this mindset, then these are the key habits I have cultivated over decades:

> Start with the right attitude; put in skillful efforts; always pay attention; never quit; face fears head on; keep it simple; focus only on what you can control; customize rituals; be balanced; always aspire to customize what works the best for you.

Now it is time to say goodbye. I trust you coming "running with me" and covering various miles via these pages left you in good shape.

We all will one day be running marathons—mental marathons, because life can be hard, and as I experienced in 2020, life can be so hard that it almost becomes unbearable.

One of the all-time bestselling books on the New York Times bestsellers list has a name *The Road Less Travelled*.

The very first sentence in that books reminds us that…life is HARD.

What a downer to some; what a reminder of reality to those who pay attention.

Perhaps you picked this book up off a shelf in a bookstore. Maybe you ordered it online. Perhaps a friend suggested you read it. I am glad to have met you. Your timing is perfect.

In this book I wanted to share ideas on how to endure life. Life is hard. It is uncertain. It can be cruel. And yet those who endure, with patience, almost always get to the goal. Never believe that your situation is hopeless. Stay in the race. Walk if you cannot run. Crawl if you cannot walk.

When I finished my 100th marathon, crossing the finish line with my wife and four kids who joined me for the last 100 yards, I thought that I might have some ideas that may help. Ideas on how to set goals and ideas on how to persist. How to cultivate resilience. How to never drop out.

Little did I know while this book was crafted that the narrative would dramatically and suddenly change.

One of my four children is no longer with us. His name is Ben. He was 16 years old at the time of his passing. His endurance did not end well. He ended his life on the first day of 2020—a year I suspected would be a year of perfect vision. Ben lost his brave battle with depression on New Year's Eve. Little did we anticipate how those early hours of the first day 2020 would change the trajectory of our lives forever in every way possible. Absolutely nothing has been the same since that fateful night.

2020 ended up indeed as a year of perfect vision. Just not the vision I had in mind. I saw clearly how his battle with depression and his hopelessness led to his demise. Life is hard. But it is also beautiful because ever since we discovered his lifeless body, we have been sustained by the love of God… day-by-day-by-day.

Maybe a future book will simply be called *Sustained*. I hope you may get to read it. Though it is not yet written I have an intuitive knowing that it will be good because it will give hope to all who suffered a major loss.

So often in life we try to make sense of our setbacks and yet I discovered that there is a time to stop doing that and engage in *radical* surrender to the fact that it is so and cannot be otherwise.

This simple and sincere book, from my heart to yours, is called *101 Finish Lines*. Please join me as we all use our various challenges to transform us and turn us into more compassionate people.

Let us move forward *together*, knowing we are sustained by Love and when we genuinely care for one another we bring peace and light to a dark world. We live on purpose.

We honor our Creator when we become more mindful of the abundant, limitless lovingkindness, compassion, joy, and peace that *already* reside inside of us.

In the end it is not so much about the number of finish lines; it is about how we run the race and press forward to the mark of a higher calling.

In the end it is also about having a deep sense of inner peace—even when life hands us what we did not expect or desire. That state of deep serenity is personally captured for me by these words in the Serenity Prayer, written by Reinhold Neibuhr in 1926.

I remain forever amazed by how these words have passed and will continue to pass a test most marathon runners pass...the ultimate test of time.

SERENITY PRAYER*

God grant me the Serenity to accept the things I cannot change
The courage to change the things I can,
And the wisdom to know the difference.
Living one day at a time,
Enjoying one moment at a time,
Accepting hardships as the pathway to peace;
Taking as He did, this sinful world as it is. Not as I would have it.

THE END

---

* For a complete version of the Serenity prayer see : www.prayerfoundation.org/dailyoffice/serenity_prayer_full_version.htm

SUMMARY OF REFLECTIONS DURING THE QUEST TO COMPLETE AT LEAST 101 MARATHONS

A

--The difference between one and 101 finish lines comes down to one word: attitude...be in charge of cultivating a healthy attitude, p. 3.

-- Always pay close attention even when you never cross railway lines, p. 42.

-- Stay accountable but make sure of two things: always make sure the mirror does not distort reality and be sure that those you choose to be open with are trustworthy, p. 54.

--Although it is 100% certain we will all age and none of us will escape death...the truth is that we have some influence in slowing down our aging process, p. 57.

--Accept the fact that few things stay the same and that we live in an imperfect world. By refusing to accept this we cause our own suffering, p. 75.

-- Watch out for the second arrows; dodge them...or better...do not fire them off toward yourself, p. 126

--If we forget to pay attention to small things in life, they can add up and cause floods of troubles. Remember to remember, p. 128.

--Every experienced marathon runner at some point misses a mark and either drops out or runs slower than expected. The great ones *always* come back and try again, p. 182.

B

--Find out where you belong; be there as often as possible....and it may just save a few lives, p. 68.

--Stay in balance, p. 94.

--Make it a point to fertilize your brain daily and do it purposefully and with joy, p. 99.

--Always do your best and surrender the outcome to a Higher Power, p. 135.

--Every morning when you wake up, take a deep breath, and know that as you breathe in, somewhere on the planet, another person is taking in a final breath, p. 189.

C

--Never compete or compare, p. 8.

--Know the customized cargo you are designed to deliver and do it with wisdom and compassion, p. 29.

--When you see enough co-incidences, consider if synchronicity may be true, p. 44.

--To sustain a certain pace of living, remember the value of cross training, p. 102.

--Do not cling to what no longer serves you, p. 195.

--Cultivate a deep sense of self-compassion and understanding that some things we control, while others we can never in a million years control or change, p. 228.

--When you know what to do...do it. Sometimes there are no second chances, p. 238.

D

--Now is the time to decide how deep you want to dive and lean into what matters the most to you, p. 16.

--Stay patient in drought seasons, because that which will arise, also will pass at some point, p. 18.

--On the outside we may all be different, but on the inside a brain is a brain and a heart is a heart, and we all bleed bright red blood when we are cut, p. 73.

--Some of my best friends are dentists, but I tell them not to take it personally when I say I prefer to see them only for routine check-ups, p. 92.

--Imitate a dog by showing enthusiasm and unconditional love, p. 248.

E

--Don't listen only to experts; also listen to your own heart or gut-instinct, p. 18.

--When we encourage others and do it to help them, make sure that the encouragement is based on reality and not false hope, p. 78.

--Pay close attention to what you eat; way more than the daily steps you take, p. 111.

--Know when enough is enough, p. 164.

--It may seem that we reach goals on our own, but the reality is that we are interconnected with others. You are never alone, p. 71.

J

--Stay in control of your own inner peace and happiness and do not allow people and circumstances to dictate your joy or steal your power, p. 151.

--See the jitters of life as hidden opportunities which teach us to become stronger, p. 172.

K

-- Learn from kids. We think we are there to teach them when the reality is that we can learn much *from* them, p. 240.

L

--There are times when one learns the most by exploring new opportunities with curiosity, p. 22.

--Never miss an opportunity to learn from another traveler, p. 46.

--The biggest need is to feel loved and to make sure we let others know we love them, p. 192.

--Be thankful for what you had…rather than focusing on your loss, p. 253.

M

--When you plan special moments make sure you do it in style, p. 12.

--It is not a matter of whether things will happen along the way; they will, p. 27.

--Every mind needs to go to the mental gym. Find a mental coach to initiate training and then consistently cultivate resilience, p. 116.

--Mindfulness is simply the skill to pay attention, p. 154.

--Let go of memories which no longer have a purpose in your life, p. 195.

-- It has been said that love makes the world go round, but may I add that in addition to love, the global appeal of great music comes in a close second, p. 206.

-- We can choose how we record memories. May I suggest you add a pen to your photos, p. 213.

--Choose to live by the meanwhile principle. It says that there is indeed a negative somewhere, but meanwhile, I will count all the other positives, p. 215.

--Make the most of every opportunity and appreciate what you have in the moment, p. 218.

--We do not always know the motives of others. We can only focus on how we perceive things and trust that others will know their own true motives, p. 243.

N

--Two universal needs are the needs to be happy and to be free of suffering. Let us always remember that whenever we encounter any stranger, p. 10,.

--Figure out what your own, unique nourishment looks like. Then follow that path consistently, p. 209.

O

-- Some opportunities indeed are once-in-a lifetime. Grab them while you can, p. 33.

--Be mindful and remember, above all, your own 99.99%, p. 146.

P

--Peace in the middle of uncertainty is possible, but like a garden, inner peace needs to be consciously and consistently cultivated, p. 31.

--Know when and how to be fully present, p. 62.

--Perfect love never fails to get rid of fear, p. 174.

--Stay very patient with myself and be comfortable with the real me. We all are works in progress, p. 202.

--I can choose if I want to be peaceful inside regardless of what is happening to me, p. 223.

--When the road forks...first pause before you choose which fork to take, p. 225.

--If your life were a picture, would it cause some to pause and feel the energy it radiates, p. 250.

Q

--It is not a matter of if things will happen along the way; they will. It's a matter of when. When that moment arrives...what is your plan? Mine is to never quit., p. 25

R

--Run only a distance that resonates with your own preferences, p. 8.

--After you put in the effort, take time to relax. Savor every moment with a loved one, if possible, p. 24.

--Rest before you get tired, p. 82.

--Role models must pass the test of time, p. 105.

-- If we forget to pay attention to small things in life, they can add up and cause floods of troubles. Remember to remember, p. 128.

-- When your life takes you in unchartered territory, relax and trust your training. Fear may want to remind you of the facts. Ignore it, p. 184.

--I have observed that one of the key differences between successful and mediocre lives has to do with the quality of morning rituals, p. 211.

--We all get multiple invitations to choose how we want to respond or react, p. 221.

-- When looking at rainbows do not think of the pot of gold at the end; think of the symbolism it represents—the faithfulness of a Creator, p. 260.

S

--The tallest trees in a forest once began as a small seed. Uncertain how things may end, we still must plant a seed, p. xvii.

--Use your sense of smell to take you back, p. 20.

--When all is obviously not ok, do your best to alleviate suffering, p. 52.

--Sit but not too long, and move but not too much, p. 94.

--Yogi Berra was 100% correct: 90% of my success so far has been all mental, p. 119.

--Wait for things to settle down, and once that happens, try to see clearly, p. 148.

--There are indeed seasons to our lives. No season lasts forever, p. 167.

--Savor what lies ahead, p. 170.

--Switch to a channel that serves you better, p. 177.

--Step by step we arrive at goals that matter to us. Savor the journey, one step at a time, p. 187.

--Do not allow yourself to feed off the scraps falling from the table. You are worthy to take a seat at the table, p. 199.

--When you buy a shoe that is your size you still have to try it on to make sure it fits, p. 231.

--The sky is the daily bread of the soul, p. 258.

--When you find more postcards with cloudy skies, than bright sunshine, the next time you are at a tourist shop...please contact me, p. 267.

T

--Trust but verify, p. 5.

--Turbulence on flights may be the same for all passengers, but each person gets to decide how they want to navigate life's sudden and unexpected turbulences, p. 35.

--Life can be simplified when we remember we have only two teachers—love or fear. My favorite teacher is the Voice of Love, p. 49.

--If you get a lot of green lights be thankful. If you get a lot of red lights be thankful too. They offer you a pause to practice intentional gratitude, p. 60.

--At a time when technology has a more ubiquitous impact on our lives, it is wise to remember to trust it, but only up to a point, p. 90.

--All of us are really in some form of training as long as we are alive, p. 102.

--Deliberately guard against the two terrible thieves of joy—also known as comparing and competing, p. 138.

-- Your thoughts always precede an action. It is a forerunner. Cultivate diamond thoughts daily, p. 140.

--To everything under the sun there is a perfect timing. Stay open and alert to recognizing the key moments, p. 161.

--Every test we are given has a beginning and an end. The low tide always makes way for the high tide, p.179.

--Travel lightly, p. 197.

U

--Our tomorrows will always be uncertain, p. 159.

--The Universe is somehow providing in ways we shall never fully understand, p. 164.

V

--Incorporate more plant-based foods on a daily basis, and if possible, see for yourself if you can be a full-time vegan, p. 109.

W

--When you hit the wall...demolish it, p. 121.

-- Next time you are upset when things don't work out, remember that you do not control it all. Blowing against the wind is a waste of energy, p. 123.

--Some walls are real, and others are imagined. Be wise to know the difference and prepare at the right pace, p. 132.

Y

--See for yourself. And then run or walk in ways that serve you well, p. 233.

ACKNOWLEGEMENTS

Writing a book is a bit like training for and running a marathon. It can be lonely at times. It tests one's endurance; unexpected obstacles arise; some stages are easy and smooth and then suddenly they become rough and one wonders *why am I doing this?*

This book would not have been possible if it were not for my wife and best friend, Corinne. Her editing skills set the bar high at times. I joked with my friends that she ran out of red ink. But her heart was always pure and at the end she gave me a hug and said "I think people will like your book."

It is really *our* book. We raised four children. As I mentioned in the book, children are our teachers. I know this as a dad and pediatrician. I see it daily in my clinic. One of our children died unexpectedly. It forever changed our family's lives. Our lives are never normal now. But we endure toward another finish line, way more important than the 101 finish lines described in this book. A deep gratitude goes out to my children: Katie, Matt, Jon, and Ben.

My hope is that this book will inspire many to maintain a skillful attitude toward life with all its ups and downs. When I hear the word "Attitude" I cannot help but be thankful to the late Dr. Jerry Jampolsky, founder of Attitudinal Healing, who taught me so much about our attitudes. Jerry called me after we lost our youngest child to suicide. Jerry taught me to live my life in ways that I am making inner peace my only goal. A huge thank you goes out to Trish Ellis for making it possible to talk to Jerry.

Alan Cohen, my coach and mentor taught me to tune in to the Voice of Love. Alan's calm demeanor teaches me to be calm in the marathon of life.

Coach Grant got me to Boston—twice. Grant taught me that less is more, and effortless exercise is possible.

My spiritual mentors Pastors Len Zoeteman, Ray Matheson and Randy Carter together with Rabbi Matusof have taught me how to be sustained by the Love of God while I endure more marathons. These men do not run marathons, but they walk the talk.

And while on the topic of men, my Pursuit Forum, has helped me to look into the mirror. Gentleman we have a confidentiality agreement, and you know who you are. Thank you for allowing me to join the tribe as we together pursue our callings.

And finally I have to acknowledge that without the role model of Jesus Christ I would not have been able to get to 101 Finish Lines. I am sustained.

ABOUT THE AUTHOR

Dr. Peter Nieman is a physician, holistic wellness coach, a marathon runner, a health journalist, and the author of *Moving Forward: The Power of Consistent Choices in Everyday Life*. Since finishing medical school in 1979, he has always disciplined himself to live life by example and aspired to find a healthy balance based upon the three foundations: spirit, soul, and body.

He appeared as a medical contributor on local and national television and has written regular medical columns for Canada's national newspaper and also the Calgary Herald.

He is married to Corinne, a family doctor, and together they have been privileged to raise four children.

Peter lives close to the Canadian Rockies and since 2009 he has continued in his quest to run every day of his life, sustained by Grace.

For more information visit www.drnieman.com.

Printed in the United States
by Baker & Taylor Publisher Services